T0274773

THE
PROSPERITY GOSPEL

Other Books by Thomas Storck

The Catholic Milieu

Christendom and the West: Essays on Culture, Society and History

From Christendom to Americanism and Beyond

An Economics of Justice and Charity: Catholic Social Teaching, Its Development and Contemporary Relevance

Liberalism: A Critique of Its Basic Principles and Its Various Forms (translated by Thomas Storck)

The Glory of the Cosmos: A Catholic Approach to the Natural World (edited by Thomas Storck)

Theology: Mythos or Logos? A Dialogue on Faith, Reason, and History (co-authored with John Médaille)

Seeing the World With Catholic Eyes: A Conversation with Thomas Storck

Foundations of a Catholic Political Order (2nd edition)

THE PROSPERITY GOSPEL

How Greed and Bad Philosophy
Distorted Christ's Teaching

Thomas Storck

TAN Books
Gastonia, North Carolina

Cover Design by Jordan Avery

Cover image: Christ and the young rich ruler, by Heinrich Hofmann, 1889 / Wikimedia Commons. Image is in Public Domain.

Library of Congress Control Number: 2022948073

ISBN: 978-1-5051-3038-6
Kindle ISBN: 978-1-5051-3039-3
ePUB ISBN: 978-1-5051-3040-9

Published in the United States by
TAN Books
PO Box 269
Gastonia, NC 28053
www.TANBooks.com

Printed in the United States of America

Contents

"For what doth it profit a man, if he gain the whole world, and suffer the loss of his own soul?"

—Matthew 16:26, DV

Preface

It is easy to ridicule the followers of the Prosperity Gospel, even if at the same time we might pity them. And perhaps such ridicule may have its place at times. But it is more important, because it is more fundamental, to try to understand the cultural roots of the Prosperity Gospel, the soil on which it thrives: the private interpretation of Scripture and the privatization of religion. These Protestant principles led to the separation of religion from the real business of life, divorcing these institutions, activities, and actions from their inherent purpose, which is ultimately the salvation of our souls. For if religious doctrines are seen simply as matters of private *opinion*, then not only do they have nothing to do with the serious purposes of life in this world, but the activities and institutions of life are robbed of their inherent and objective purposes. All is now a matter of private opinion. Religion then becomes merely a means of satisfying our emotional or psychological needs.

This reduction of religion to the private realm is deep-seated in our culture. The famed English historian Christopher Dawson, during his tenure as a professor at Harvard, delivered a lecture in 1960 characterizing American religion as "detached from the objective world which was the domain of business and politics . . . , so that, as several Americans have remarked to me, they find some difficulty in relating the two concepts of religion and civilization since these seem to belong to two quite distinct orders of existence."[1] This attitude of detaching religion from the real business of mankind has its theoretical justification in the writings of John Locke, and Locke in turn was enthusiastically adopted even before the American Revolution as something like our official political philosopher. The historian Louis Hartz termed Locke a "massive national cliché" who "dominates American political thought, as no thinker anywhere dominates the political thought of a nation,"[2] something most evident in the religious liberty jurisprudence of the United States Supreme Court. It is almost astounding how closely the court's opinions on religious freedom hew to the framework of Locke's ideas and simply assume the general outline of the question as Locke presents it in his writings, most notably in his (first) *Letter Concerning Toleration* of 1689. The fusion of Protestant private biblical interpretation with Locke's Enlightenment understanding of the role of religion in society has resulted in a situation where questions of meaning are relegated to private life, and the real business of living for most people becomes the pursuit of wealth, which is regarded as the obvious purpose of life. Any religious strictures against it are rejected as tainted by socialism. And in the Prosperity Gospel, it is religion itself that has come to be co-opted into serving the national infatuation with affluence. Instead of the Gospel judging, ruling, and

---

[1] Christopher Dawson, "America and the Secularization of Modern Culture," a lecture delivered at the University of Saint Thomas, Houston, Texas, 1960.

[2] Louis Hartz, *The Liberal Tradition in America* (New York: Harcourt, Brace & World, 1955), 140.

shaping our desires and passions, it becomes the other way around: our disordered desires now determine the contents of the Gospel itself, and we end up with a situation which, as Pope Saint John Paul II put it, has led "to permissive and consumerist solutions, which under various pretexts seek to convince man that he is free from every law and from God himself, thus imprisoning him within a selfishness which ultimately harms both him and others."[3]

From this fundamental cultural basis, it is not hard to see how these attitudes have overflowed into all areas of life, for it is not just our seeking after worldly goods whose ends have been perverted, but everything that this spirit of mammon touches. Education, for example, is commonly justified by its presumed or hoped for return on investment, or more bluntly put: Does it pay? Can I use it to get rich? Any other reason is seen, frankly, as quaint at best or, at worst, stupidly naive. This book will consider first the central ideas which have shaped the culture of the United States in these respects, ideas which are certainly not unique to this country and largely did not originate here, but which have found their most fertile soil in it. Then it will examine the crucial questions of freedom and of whether and how human activities and institutions have inherent purposes, purposes beyond those which each individual might confer upon them. Then we will look at the ramifications of these ideas upon some of the activities and institutions of our society, such as the economy, education, science, and so on. Doubtless, to draw such connections will be unfamiliar territory for many readers,

---

[3] Pope John Paul II, *Centesimus Annus* (May 1, 1991), no. 55.

but I believe that such a discussion can be both interesting and enlightening, and moreover, that any other treatment of such a singular phenomenon as the Prosperity Gospel runs the risk of both superficiality and an arrogant and scornful assumption of superiority. When we behold both the Prosperity preachers and their duped followers, we should keep in mind our national cultural affinity for their bizarre doings. As the saying goes, Only in America . . .

Finally, I conclude this book with some reflections on the genuine place that material goods ought to hold in our life as Catholics. God created us with a need for such goods, and even before the Fall, God put Adam "in the garden of Eden to till it and keep it" (Gn 2:15). Therefore, the products of human work are not evil. But if we fail to see to what extent the disaster that our first parents brought upon the human race has unhinged our very selves and released our various passions from the command of reason, we will not grasp how corrupted we can be by the activities of moneymaking and consuming. Our medieval ancestors were very well aware of the need for caution in this aspect of human life, but because modern Catholics on the whole have not followed their example, we find ourselves in a situation where the whole culture has been tainted, if not corrupted, by these twin passions.

May this book contribute in some small way to the rediscovery of our pressing need to watch carefully over our possession and use of the good things of this earth so that, as the Collect for the third Sunday after Pentecost in the traditional Roman liturgy puts it, *transeamus per bona temporalia, ut non amittamus aeterna* (we may pass through temporal goods so as not to lose eternal goods).

Introduction

"Where your treasure is, there will your heart be also."

—Luke 12:34

Lakewood Church in Houston, Texas, is the congregation pastored by the Evangelical Protestant Joel Osteen, one of the most noted of the preachers of what is often called the Prosperity Gospel, the notion that God will reward believers with the good things of this life, and in particular with wealth. The fundamental error of this belief—one hesitates to call it a theology—is that the Christian life is all about me, me, me—and about fulfilling one's dreams and desires, whatever they may be. Their website minces no words: "At Lakewood we believe your best days are still out in front of you. . . . The Bible says when you are planted in the house of the Lord, you will flourish. Get ready to step into a new level of your destiny."[4] In another place, Osteen says, "Live inspired. Reach your dreams. Become all God created you to be."[5]

Paula White, another of the promoters of such a false Gospel, is equally or more explicit: "God has a plan. . . . That

---

[4] Lakewood Church (website), accessed August 23, 2022, https://www .lakewoodchurch.com/?target=/pages/give/index.aspx.

[5] Joel Osteen Ministries (website), accessed August 31, 2022, https:// live.joelosteen.com/.

plan is always working. And that plan includes you! God has a BIG LIFE for you. He has designed a life of wholeness, one that is blessed and successful, for you to enjoy—one that has peace and purpose, joy, goodness, completeness, wealth, health and fullness."[6]

But the Joel Osteens and Paula Whites of this world are not a new phenomenon, especially in the United States. They flourish on ground already well prepared for them and their message. The Baptist minister and founder of Temple University in Philadelphia, Russell Conwell (1843–1925), offered a similar message with his popular address "Acres of Diamonds," which he delivered hundreds of times in the late nineteenth and early twentieth centuries: "I say that you ought to be rich, and it is your duty to get rich. How many of my pious brethren say to me, 'Do you, a Christian minister, spend your time going up and down the country advising young people to get rich, to get money?' 'Yes, of course I do.' They say, 'Isn't that awful! Why don't you preach the gospel instead of preaching about man's making money?' 'Because to make money honestly is to preach the gospel.'"[7]

A few years later, Bruce Barton's 1925 bestseller, *The Man Nobody Knows*, portrays our Lord as "The Founder of Modern Business." The author tells us that "every one of the 'principles of modern salesmenship' on which business men so much pride themselves, are brilliantly exemplified

---

[6] "You Can Have a Big Life!" Paula White Ministries, December 30, 2020, https://paulawhite.org/news/you-can-have-a-big-life/.

[7] Russell H. Conwell, *Acres of Diamonds* (New York: Harper Brothers, 1915), 17–22.

in Jesus' talk and work," and he compares His teaching that (as Barton phrases it) "whosoever of you will be the chiefest, shall be servant of all" with the advice of one of the founders of the New York Life Insurance Company, whose idea of service was "of extending the Company's service throughout the world, of making it the finest, most useful institution of its kind." And incidentally, by doing so, "it made us rich."[8]

As time went on, this message became more detached from any Christian veneer, and it manifested more crudely what later became known as the power of positive thinking. Thus we find Napoleon Hill's 1937 volume, likewise a bestseller, *Think and Grow Rich*, a book with a considerable following still today, telling us,

> If you truly DESIRE money so keenly that your desire is an obsession, you will have no difficulty in convincing yourself that you will acquire it. The object is to want money, and to become so determined to have it that you CONVINCE yourself you will have it.
>
> Only those who become "money conscious" ever accumulate great riches. "Money consciousness" means that the mind has become so thoroughly saturated with the DESIRE for money, that one can see one's self already in possession of it.[9]

---

[8] Bruce Barton, *The Man Nobody Knows: A Discovery of the Real Jesus* (Grosset & Dunlap, 1924), https://archive.org/stream/in.ernet.dli.2015 .179576/2015.179576.The-Man-Nobody-Knows-A-Discovery-Of-The -Real-Jesus_djvu.txt.

[9] Napoleon Hill, *Think and Grow Rich* (1938), chap. 2, https://sacred -texts.com/nth/tgr/tgr07.htm.

This attitude toward wealth and getting rich should seem strange and alien to any Christian, for Holy Scripture teaches a radically different attitude. Even casual readers of the scriptural text will notice the often harsh language that the sacred writers employ about riches and the rich. We have the parable of the rich man and Lazarus (see Lk 16:19–31), Saint James's striking rebuke to the rich (see Jas 5:1–3), and Our Lord's own words, "But woe to you that are rich, for you have received your consolation" (Lk 6:24). In one of the most famous of such passages, Saint Paul warns us against the pursuit of riches with these words: "If we have food and clothing, with these we shall be content. But those who desire to be rich fall into temptation, into a snare, into many senseless and hurtful desires that plunge men into ruin and destruction. For the love of money is the root of all evils; it is through this craving that some have wandered away from the faith and pierced their hearts with many pangs" (1 Tm 6:8–10).[10]

It is often pointed out that the Apostle is not condemning money itself nor even the possession of money, but "the love of money." Quite true. But the point is that money and the goods that money can buy are themselves temptations, for "those who desire to be rich fall into temptation." Great wealth is a classic example of what Catholic moral theology calls a near occasion of sin. Certainly there are those who are rich yet who are detached from their money and their possessions. But I venture to say they are a decided minority. Most of us become all too attached to our possessions, and

---

[10] For other examples, see Proverbs 23:4; Micah 6:12a; Matthew 19:24; Luke 1:53b.

often the more possessions, the greater the attachment. "The spirit of poverty is far more rare among the rich than among the poor. Saint Thomas Aquinas compares, as two things equally extraordinary, Abraham's freedom of heart in the midst of all his riches, and Samson's victory over the Philistines, with the ass's jawbone as his only weapon."[11]

Even using a calculation based solely on self-interest, we would be foolish to ignore these words of Sacred Scripture, which is the inspired Word of God. At one point, Our Lord asked the pointed question, "For what doth it profit a man, if he gain the whole world, and suffer the loss of his own soul?" (Matt. 16:26, DV). And for anyone who believes in eternal life, the answer is obvious. It would be utterly irrational to trade a mere seventy or eighty or more years on this earth spent in riches or pleasures for an eternity of separation from God, a separation that means the total frustration of our true end as rational creatures. For believers who acknowledge these truths, this kind of calculation should be clear.

At the same time, Our Lord said, "I came that they may have life, and have it abundantly" (Jn 10:10). Indeed, God desires that we live a life of fullness in this world, "a life of wholeness, one that is blessed and successful." But with a difference! Saint John Henry Newman offers a well-known meditation on this matter: "God has created me to do Him some definite service. He has committed some work to me which He has not committed to another. I have my mission.

---

[11] Pie-Raymond Régamey, *Poverty, An Essential Element in the Christian Life* (New York: Sheed & Ward, 1950), 56.

. . . He has not created me for naught. I shall do good; I shall do his work."[12]

Newman, however, significantly adds the following words: "If I am in sickness, my sickness may serve Him, in perplexity, my perplexity may serve Him. If I am in sorrow, my sorrow may serve Him. He does nothing in vain. He knows what he is about. He may take away my friends. He may throw me among strangers. He may make me feel desolate, make my spirits sink, hide my future from me. Still, He knows what He is about."[13]

Even though they both speak of finding our purpose in life, clearly Cardinal Newman and the preachers of the Prosperity Gospel do not share an understanding of God's workings in this world—that is, what it means to follow Christ. And what it means to have a mission in this world. Preachers like Joel Osteen and Paula White do not speak of serving God in sickness or perplexity or poverty or sorrow or desolation, or even of taking up one's cross and denying oneself. What they preach is simply the opposite of the Christian spiritual life. And their glib references to Scripture are mere window dressing for a secular, this-worldly message of preoccupation with self and with a happiness that consists in the good things of this world.

Catholics are not Manicheans. We do not consider material goods as sinful. But we recognize, or should recognize,

---

[12] John Henry Newman, *Meditations and Devotions of the Late Cardinal Newman*, ed. William Paine Neville (London: Longmans, Green, 1907). Available on the web at numerous places, including https://www.john henrynewmancatholiccollege.org.uk/john-henry-newman-prayers/.

[13] Newman, *Meditations and Devotions.*

two facts: First, that our earthly life must be subordinate to our eternal life, and a use of earthly goods that makes the acquisition of eternal life more difficult is at the very least an occasion of sin. Second, that the goods of this world have a purpose. We need them both to survive as well as to live a truly human life. God did not intend for us to live as hunter gatherers or cave dwellers. But having attained a sufficient level of human goods, it is not merely foolish to want more, but to the extent that such goods are an obstacle to our attainment of eternal life, they are in truth harmful to us.

Saint Augustine compared our life on this earth to a journey to our true home: "We find, however, that we must make use of some mode of conveyance, either by land or water, in order to reach that fatherland where our enjoyment is to commence. But the beauty of the country through which we pass, and the very pleasure of the motion, charm our hearts, and turning these things which we ought to use into objects of enjoyment, we become unwilling to hasten the end of our journey; and becoming engrossed in a false delight, our thoughts are diverted from that home whose delights would make us truly happy."[14]

If we take a vacation, it is not wrong to enjoy our accommodations along the way. But if we forget our destination in our enjoyment of what is meant to be simply a stop on the way to that destination, then we have exchanged means for ends. Of course, in something as comparatively unimportant as a vacation, we can, if we choose, decide we like

---

[14] Augustine, *On Christian Doctrine*, trans. J. F. Shaw, in *Great Books of the Western World*, vol. 18 (Chicago: Encyclopaedia Britannica, c. 1952), 625. I have made some alteration to this translation.

the hotel pool better than the seaside resort we originally set out for, but between heaven and earth, we do not have the liberty of making such an exchange. Our destination is fixed for us. Whether we like it or not, every day we are journeying toward eternity.

The Catholic ideal involves properly subordinating our temporal interests to those of eternity. Catholics do not deny that the goods of this world are real goods worth seeking and possessing, but we should only pursue them according to the measure in which they serve a truly human life and do not hinder our attainment of eternal life. The Prosperity Gospel and the materialism ingrained in American culture from which it arose and in which it thrives see the goods of this world as ends in themselves, as having little or no connection with anything beyond them. But this, as we have seen, is false.

But if the blandishments of the Prosperity Gospel find such ready acceptance in this country, why is this so? How and why have the promoters of worldly prosperity, such as Joel Osteen or Paula White and their earlier brethren such as Russell Conwell or Bruce Barton or Napoleon Hill, arisen? Where did they come from and why? In the rest of this book, we will consider this question and the related subject of the effects of their beliefs on the variety of human activities, including the economy, science, education, and the arts, as well as what is the proper Catholic response.

CHAPTER ONE

Culture: Protestant or Catholic

Most Catholics would smile at the naive worldliness of Joel Osteen or Russell Conwell. As the Church founded by Christ, who Himself rejected the first anti-gospel preacher, the devil in the desert, we are not so apt to fall for such blatant distortions of the Gospel of Jesus Christ. As Saint Matthew's Gospel declares, "Again, the devil took him to a very high mountain, and showed him all the kingdoms of the world and the glory of them; and he said to him, 'All these I will give you, if you will fall down and worship me.' Then Jesus said to him, 'Begone, Satan! for it is written, "You shall worship the Lord your God and him only shall you serve"'" (4:8–10). False promises of earthly wealth and glory were quickly repelled by Christ. We are too rooted in Christian tradition and the wisdom of the saints to listen to such diabolical whispers of prosperity. But we should not be so sure that we ourselves are immune from these sorts of tendencies. For the influence of the surrounding Protestant culture upon American Catholics has been immense, and one of the most noteworthy characteristics of that culture is its affection for wealth.

Before looking at that specific point of the relationship between Protestant culture and moneymaking, we should first consider what culture is and how a particular culture shapes those who live within it. The word *culture*, as meaning something like "A common way of life—a particular adjustment of man to his natural surroundings and his economic needs," and which is "based on a social tradition . . . embodied in its institutions, its literature and its art,"[15] is relatively recent in Western thought, becoming current only in the second half of the nineteenth century. As one philosopher pointed out, "a few centuries ago this wide meaning of the word would have made no sense to any audience."[16] But although the term itself is recent, the concept is not, and the same meaning was often expressed less succinctly by previous writers. For *culture* does correspond to something both real and important, and this is shown by its frequent use by a number of important Catholic writers, as we will see shortly.

Using this understanding of culture as "a common way of life," we can see that all human beings are born and brought up within a particular culture. And this culture has an enormous influence on how we think and act. It is true that we are not trapped within our cultures and that, with sufficient effort, we can see beyond the particular vision of life that our own culture proposes, but it is also true that most of us do not make much of an effort to do so. Thus when we are born

---

[15] Christopher Dawson, *The Dynamics of World History* (La Salle, IL: Sherwood Sugden, 1978), 4, 104.

[16] T. Viik, "What About the Philosophy of Culture?," *Acta Philosophica Fennica* 65 (2000): 247.

into a culture, for the most part, we imbibe its vices along with its virtues, its errors along with its truths.

Numerous observers with differing views have noted the United States' preoccupation with money and material goods. For example, in his 1889 book *The Question of Nationality in its Relation to the Catholic Church*, Fr. Anton Walburg, a Cincinnati priest of German background, wrote, "The ideal set before every American youth is money. Money is not only needful, but is the one thing needful. Money is a power everywhere, but here it is the supreme power. . . . In Europe, a man enjoys his competence; but here, no one has enough."[17]

And half a century earlier, the famous French commentator Alexis de Tocqueville wrote of Americans that "one usually finds that love of money is either the chief or a secondary motive at the bottom of everything the Americans do," and, "The American will describe as noble and estimable ambition that which our medieval ancestors would have called base cupidity."[18] And for a more recent example, the American economist John Kenneth Galbraith wrote some interesting words on this enduring American attitude toward wealth and material things.

> In the autumn of 1954, during the Congressional elections of that year, the Republicans replied to Democratic attacks on their stewardship by arguing that this was the second best year in history. It was not,

---

[17] In Aaron Abell, ed., *American Catholic Thought on Social Questions* (Indianapolis: Bobbs-Merrill, 1968), 40, 41, 43.

[18] Alexis de Tocqueville, *Democracy in America*, trans. J. P. Mayer (Garden City, NY: Anchor Books, 1969), 615, 621.

in all respects, a happy defense. Many promptly said that second best was not good enough—certainly not for Americans. But no person in either party showed the slightest disposition to challenge the standard by which it is decided that one year is better than another. Nor was it felt that any explanation was required. No one would be so eccentric as to suppose that second best meant second best in the progress of the arts and the sciences. No one would assume that it referred to health, education, or the battle against juvenile delinquency. . . . Despite a marked and somewhat ostensible preoccupation with religious observances at the time, no one was moved to suppose that 1954 was the second best year as measured by the number of people who had found enduring spiritual solace.

Second best could mean only one thing—that the production of goods was the second highest in history. There had been a year in which production was higher and which hence was better. In fact in 1954 the Gross National Product was $360.5 billion; the year before it had been $364.5. This measure of achievement was acceptable to all. . . . On the importance of production there is no difference between Republicans and Democrats, right and left, white or colored, Catholic or Protestant.[19]

"On the importance of production there is no difference between . . . Catholic or Protestant." If Catholics, then, are

[19] John Kenneth Galbraith, *The Affluent Society* (New York: Mentor, 1958), 101.

more apt to reject the crude manifestations of the Prosperity Gospel as illustrated by Joel Osteen and Paula White, how is it that we are just as likely to see production or wealth as the obvious standard by which we judge whether a year or a country is better or worse? The answer lies in the overwhelmingly Protestant culture and its influence on the millions of Catholic immigrants from Europe or Latin America or elsewhere. To understand this better, we need to examine the relationship between religion and culture. Although culture is a common way of life based on an adjustment to environment and passed on to succeeding generations, it is more than this. Every culture is based on a religion, or on some secular substitute for religion. When the Catholic Middle East was seized by Muslims in the seventh century, the physical environment did not change, but the culture changed profoundly because a new religious impulse was implanted there. And when much of northern Europe broke away from Catholic unity in the sixteenth century, likewise a new culture arose in those countries. For the Protestant religion, like all religions, produced a definite type of culture, a culture in which a preoccupation with wealth and material goods came to hold a more prominent place than in Catholic cultures, or even in cultures historically formed by Catholicism.

In the early 1930s, Hilaire Belloc set forth clearly the act of the existence of these competing cultures in his seminal essay "The Two Cultures of the West": "There is a Protestant culture and a Catholic culture. The difference between these two is the main difference dividing one sort of European from another. The boundary between the Catholic and

Protestant cultures is *the* great line of cleavage, compared with which all others are secondary."[20]

And this "great line of cleavage" is the sign of something important and fundamental—namely, of a culture's understanding of the Divine Nature itself. As Catholic British Historian Christopher Dawson once declared, "In the last resort every civilization is built on a religious foundation: it is the expression in social institutions and cultural activity of a faith or a vision of reality which gives the civilization its spiritual unity."[21] Pope Saint John Paul II also expressed this same point in a striking passage in his encyclical *Centesimus Annus.*

> It is not possible to understand the human person on the basis of economics alone, nor to define the person simply on the basis of class membership. A human being is understood in a more complete way when situated within the sphere of culture through language, history, and the position one takes towards the fundamental events of life, such as birth, love, work and death. At the heart of every culture lies the attitude a person takes to the greatest mystery: the mystery of God. Different cultures are basically different ways of facing the question of the meaning of personal existence.[22]

---

[20] Hilaire Belloc, "The Two Cultures of the West," in *Essays of a Catholic* (Rockford, IL: TAN Books, 1992), 239.

[21] Christopher Dawson, *Understanding Europe* (Garden City, NY: Image, 1960), 211.

[22] Pope John Paul II, *Centismus Annus* (May 1, 1991), no. 24.

The theological differences between the Catholic faith and the various Protestant groups extend far beyond particular points of doctrine, for these theological differences imply and foster different approaches to both understanding and living our lives in this world. G. K. Chesterton made some very perceptive remarks on how Protestant theology manifested itself in unexpected ways.

> A Puritan meant originally a man whose mind had no holidays. To use his own favourite phrase, he would let no living thing come between him and his God; an attitude which involved eternal torture for him and a cruel contempt for all the living things. It was better to worship in a barn than in a cathedral for the specific and specified reason that the cathedral was beautiful. Physical beauty was a false and sensual symbol coming in between the intellect and the object of its intellectual worship. . . .
>
> This is the essential Puritan idea, that God can only be praised by direct contemplation of Him. You must praise God only with your brain; it is wicked to praise Him with your passions or your physical habits or your gesture or instinct of beauty. Therefore it is wicked to worship by singing or dancing or drinking sacramental wines or building beautiful churches or saying prayers when you are half asleep . . . we can only worship by thinking. Our heads can praise God, but never our hands and feet.[23]

---

[23] G. K. Chesterton, *George Bernard Shaw* (New York: John Lane, 1909), 43.

This, incidentally, is the reason that Protestants generally pray with their eyes closed, whereas Catholics can pray either way, and perhaps most often with eyes open. And so these "different ways of facing the question of the meaning of personal existence" can manifest themselves in surprising ways, not merely in what we formally believe or how we worship. As the late Fr. George Bull, philosophy professor at Fordham University, once keenly noted, "In recent years, Catholics have become increasingly conscious of the clash between Catholicism as a *general* culture, and the culture of the world around them. The work of men like Belloc, Maritain, Christopher Dawson and others, has shown that we differ not in religion alone, but in the whole realm of unspoken and spontaneous things, which color even our daily routine."[24]

Although there are many differences between cultures formed by the Faith and those formed by one or another sort of Protestantism, Catholics in the United States are surrounded by an oppressive Protestant culture. Even well catechized Catholics—as perhaps a majority of American Catholics were in the first half of the last century—continue to drink from their polluted surroundings. Consequently, their attitudes will then negatively shape their daily activities and practices. Formal religious instruction necessarily deals with the sublime truths of the Faith, truths about God and His Church, the means of grace, salvation, and so on. Religious instruction also deals with obvious violations of the

---

[24] George Bull, "The Function of the Catholic Graduate School," *Thought* 13, no. 3 (September 1938).

Ten Commandments, what we must do or avoid in order to attain to salvation. But such religious instruction rarely or never considers how these truths of faith and morals express themselves in "the sphere of culture," outside of things such as marriage and family. Beyond these, our cultural traits are usually seen as things that are indifferent, instead of as manifestations of our deepest religious outlook.

In another passage from John Paul's encyclical *Centesimus Annus*, the pope points out the way that cultural attitudes toward material goods reflect in fact our deepest beliefs about God and the world which He created. In a passage discussing the varying responses made after World War II to Communist materialism, he speaks of one attempt to defeat Communism as

> the affluent society or the consumer society. It seeks to defeat Marxism on the level of pure materialism by showing how a free-market society can achieve a greater satisfaction of material human needs than Communism, while equally excluding spiritual values. In reality, while on the one hand it is true that this social model shows the failure of Marxism to contribute to a humane and better society, on the other hand, insofar as it denies an autonomous existence and value to morality, law, culture and religion, it agrees with Marxism, in the sense that it totally reduces man to the sphere of economics and the satisfaction of material needs.[25]

---

[25] Pope John Paul II, *Centesimus Annus*, no. 19.

Thus the fact that American Catholics in 1954 had no problem with equating "best" with the greatest "production of goods" should be a warning to us that we have absorbed much from our cultural surroundings that is at odds with the Faith we profess.

So while Catholics in the United States mostly reject the crudities of the Prosperity Gospel preachers, I am afraid that we usually neither perceive nor reject the cultural or societal background from which these preachers of personal prosperity have arisen and in which they flourish. We too, as Galbraith affirmed, tend to accept that increased production is always better and that acquiring worldly possessions is an unqualified good and the primary social criterion of better and worse. As early as 1869, the Catholic attorney and politician Charles O'Connor of New York City wrote, "In worn out, king ridden Europe, men must stay where they are born, but in America, a man is accounted a failure, and ought to be, who has not risen above his father's station in life."[26]

Even if we confess in theory that the pursuit of riches can be dangerous, do we not in fact contradict this by the way we live our lives? Do we not in fact agree by our actions with O'Connor that "a man is accounted a failure, and ought to be, who has not risen above his father's station in life"? Are not most of us happy if our children are admitted to a prestigious college that will open numerous lucrative personal contacts, even though the Faith is not taught there, and students are hardly known for their Christian moral conduct? Or if they enter upon a career likely to make them rich,

---

[26] Quoted in Daniel J. O'Brien, *Public Catholicism*, 2nd ed. (Maryknoll: Orbis, 1996), 62.

paying no heed to Saint Paul's warnings that the mere "desire to be rich" leads many "into temptation, into a snare, into many senseless and hurtful desires that plunge men into ruin and destruction"? (1 Tm 6:9). Do we not largely ignore the possibility that our children and we ourselves risk eternal separation from God for the sake of worldly riches?

In what is probably the most widely-used economics textbook in the world, Paul Samuelson posits as one of the bases of his entire understanding of economics the alleged desire of everyone, at least every American, to become rich: "An objective observer would have to agree that, even after two centuries of rapid economic growth, production in the United States is simply not high enough to meet everyone's desires. If you add up all the wants, you quickly find that there are simply not enough goods and services to satisfy even a small fraction of everyone's consumption desires. Our national output would have to be many times larger before the average American could live at the level of the average doctor or big-league baseball player."[27]

Does the United States' economy produce "enough goods and services" so that no one need live in poverty? Can we satisfy pretty much everyone's *reasonable* desires for external goods? Certainly, yes, and if the discipline of economics is not content with that as a goal, then I submit that it is as much at odds with Holy Scripture and Christian tradition as would be a kind of psychology that promoted the unrestricted satisfaction of sexual desires with equally spurious arguments.

---

[27] Paul Samuelson, *Microeconomics*, 17th ed. (Boston: McGraw-Hill Irwin, 2001), 4.

In his remarkable book *Mont-Saint-Michel and Chartres*, Henry Adams, the grandson and great-grandson of two American presidents, pointed out, "Just as the French of the nineteenth century invested their surplus capital in a railway system in the belief that they would make money by it in this life, in the thirteenth they trusted their money to the Queen of Heaven because of their belief in her power to repay it with interest in the life to come."[28]

How much money was entrusted to the Queen of Heaven and for what? "According to statistics, in the single century between 1170 and 1270, the French built eighty cathedrals and nearly five hundred churches of the cathedral class, which would have cost, according to an estimate made in 1840, more than five thousand millions to replace. Five thousand million francs is a thousand million dollars, and this covered only the great churches of a single century."[29]

And this by a society much poorer than ours, one that is often criticized, even by Catholics, for its poverty and failure to promote worldly success. "Where your treasure is, there will your heart be also" (Mt 6:21), Our Lord said on one occasion. Without a doubt, the Middle Ages and the modern world have two different hearts as revealed by the construction of their monuments. Shopping malls, amusement parks, sports arenas, massive highway systems for massive vehicles, McMansions—these are where we as a society invest our money, trusting not in heaven's Queen but in the demon Mammon. And by and large we modern Catholics

---

[28] Henry Adams, *Mont-Saint-Michel and Chartres* (New York: Gallery Books, 1985), 65.
[29] Adams, 65.

have embraced an alien scale of values, utterly changing our attitudes toward the use of money. While we might occasionally make utterances about the dangers of riches and materialism, in fact we have accepted the attitude toward material goods that our society around us holds, and the unlimited pursuit of wealth is generally seen by Catholics as an entirely legitimate activity, apparently free from all dangers to our eternal salvation. The harsh words in Scripture about the rich and their wealth are seldom attended to and facilely explained away by such techniques as I pointed out above, distinguishing between *money* and *the love of money*: true as far as it goes, but hardly to the point.

If we admit Belloc's point that "there is a Protestant culture and a Catholic culture," and that "the difference between these two is the main difference dividing one sort of European from another," then we must ask: How did the Protestant culture of this country come to embody an attitude such that "one usually finds that love of money is either the chief or a secondary motive at the bottom of everything the Americans do"? How did the likes of Joel Osteen and Paula White find such fertile soil in this country, persons whose message and whose entire behavior and demeanor would have seemed simply ridiculous, at least historically, even to Protestant Christians in Europe?

On one level, the disordered desire for riches is present in the heart of every person. Hence the harsh warnings about the pursuit of riches in Holy Scripture, both in those addressed originally to the Hebrews themselves and those of the New Testament intended chiefly for gentile converts. In this respect, Americans are neither worse nor better than others. We all share equally in the effects of original sin. But if this is so, how comes it that in this country, this hankering for wealth is more common, more obvious, and more acceptable to public opinion than it is elsewhere? The answer lies in the exclusive cultural omnipresence of Protestantism in this country, in the absence of those cultural restraints which historically tended to check these desires.

Every European country has a Catholic past. But not the United States. It is true that the Protestant settlers of the thirteen original colonies were all physically descended from Catholics, but *as a society*, we have no shared Catholic past. In Europe, on the other hand, it is impossible to ignore the Catholic past. On an obvious but relatively superficial level, there are physical monuments of Catholicism everywhere. Whether we are speaking of ruined monasteries or church buildings appropriated by Protestants and perhaps still in use today, it is a fact impossible to deny that these physical remains testify to the former omnipresence of the Catholic Church and Catholic culture.

More important than these physical reminders, of course, each European country received an original Catholic cultural stamp, a stamp that in many cases, despite decades or even centuries of apostasy, is still perceptible and exercises a certain force. But the United States never had a corporate Catholic character. Our culture, from our intellectual life to our everyday folkways, was shaped by a Protestantism unrestrained by any corporate historical memory of a Catholic past. The United States, as a newly-constituted Protestant society, even before the Revolution, had no Catholic past to repudiate since it had no shared Catholic past at all.

Of course, it is true that certain elements of cultural life were holdovers from Catholic ages. We inherited, for example, English common law, a creation of Catholic ages. But such fragments of a Catholic past, displaced in any case from their place in a Catholic culture as a whole, did not serve to counteract the powerful effects of the new doctrines, embraced with such zeal, especially by the American colonials, and most especially by those who set the intellectual and spiritual tone of the new settlements.

Thus a new society was formed, a *Novus Ordo Seclorum* (a New Order of the Ages), as the Great Seal of the United States proclaims. And equally important as the lack of a shared Catholic past was the privatizing of religion. On a political level, the First Amendment to the newly-written Constitution effectively rendered religion a private matter in this country; for society as a whole, organized politically, religion, and especially dogmatic religious truth, was of no concern. Religion was recognized certainly as a sociological fact and a very helpful aid to social order, but not as a possible source of truth. Of course, despite this official neglect of dogmatic religion, the country's culture was Protestant. The legal and political regime reinforced the tendency already present in Protestantism to make religion a wholly private affair. Religion was one thing; public life another.

Stemming from its Protestant roots, religion in America assumed a peculiar role. Christopher Dawson wrote that "English Protestantism . . . produced a new form of culture, and indeed a new type of Christianity, which was subsequently diffused all over the world, and especially in North

America, so that it became one of the great forces that have shaped the modern world."[30]

But what was this "new form of culture" or "new type of Christianity"? Dawson spoke of this in a lecture he delivered in 1960: "Thus American religion was detached from the objective world which was the domain of business and politics and focused on the subjective world of religious feeling—above all the intense experience of religious conversion. This, I believe, has left a permanent mark on the American mind, so that, as several Americans have remarked to me, they find some difficulty in relating the two concepts of religion and civilization since these seem to belong to two quite distinct orders of existence."[31]

The preoccupation with "the subjective world of religious feeling" was a result of privatizing religion, which in turn strengthened that tendency, raising a wall of separation between religion and "the objective world which was the domain of business and politics." Consequently, actual religious doctrines are now downplayed in the United States. Religious *feeling*, what Dawson called "the subjective world of religious feeling," not the intellectual contents of belief, was what came to matter. Religion as subjective emotion was obviously something distinct from the hardheaded world of business or politics. Most people are accustomed to think that differences in religion, at least

---

[30] Christopher Dawson, *The Dividing of Christendom* (Garden City, NY: Image, 1967), 104.

[31] Christopher Dawson, "America and the Secularization of Modern Culture," a lecture delivered at the University of Saint Thomas, Houston, Texas, 1960.

among Christians, are in fact comparatively unimportant. Since religion is generally held to be a private matter, not really part of the serious business of life, which is reflected chiefly in our commercial and political activity, we are apt to regard religious preference as something akin to adherence to a favorite sports team.

Since there is little interest in religious dogma, religion is held to be chiefly or wholly a moral force, morality being here purely personal—that is, having no connection with the worlds of business or politics. The 1780 Massachusetts Constitution provided "for the institution of the public worship of God and for the support and maintenance of public Protestant teachers of piety, religion and morality" (article III). In an 1810 case concerning the right of the town of Falmouth to determine which religious bodies could receive tax funds for their support, the chief justice of Massachusetts justified the provision in the Massachusetts Constitution as follows: "The object of public religious instruction is to teach, and to enforce by suitable arguments, the practice of a system of correct morals among the people, and to form and cultivate reasonable and just habits and manners, by which every man's person and property are protected from outrage, and his personal and social enjoyments promoted and multiplied."[32] Whatever may have been the original intention of the New England settlers, by the end of the eighteenth century, the practice of government support for religion was upheld simply by moral arguments.

---

[32] Quoted in Conrad Wright, *The Unitarian Controversy* (Boston: Skinner House, 1994), 23–24.

Nor was this something peculiar to Massachusetts. Fr. Giovanni Grassi, an Italian Jesuit who served as president of Georgetown between 1812 and 1817 wrote, "[Americans] who describe themselves as members of one or another of the sects do not thereby profess an abiding adherence to the doctrines of the founders of the sect."[33]

And about a hundred years later, the German sociologist Max Weber recorded that "in the main, the congregations refused entirely to listen to the preaching of 'dogma' and to confessional distinctions. 'Ethics' alone could be offered."[34] And today, such a prominent spokesman for American Christianity as Rod Dreher, although professedly an Eastern Orthodox Christian, has explicitly subordinated questions of dogmatic truth to a vague agreement on certain currently contested moral tenets which are characteristic of, as he terms it, "conservative" Christianity.

Since American society possessed a vague Protestant veneer, the morality preached and inculcated by nearly all the religious bodies was quite similar. It was a generalized Protestant morality, although largely detached from the particular dogmatic tenets officially held by each denomination. But this morality was, as I said, purely personal and highly selective in its interest. Thus, it concerned itself to a disproportionate degree with sins against the sixth and ninth commandments or even with alcoholic consumption. At the same time, these religious bodies greatly ignored morality as it applies to the business world, especially its conduct

---

[33] Quoted in Seymour Martin Lipset, *The First New Nation* (Garden City, NY: Doubleday, 1967), 174.

[34] Lipset, 177.

towards employees or competitors or questions of justification for waging war and subsequent conduct in war. All of
these matters were divorced from morality or religion since
they were part of the "domain of business and politics," part
of the *real* world, we may say.

In fact, the morality inculcated by this generalized American religiosity had little or no interest in questions of money,
or with the desire to become rich. As a result, the preachers
of the Prosperity Gospel are not seen as violating any core
principle of Christian morality, as would be the case if they
promoted, instead of riches, unrestricted and unlimited sexual enjoyment. They cater to our desire for riches, something
which is not usually seen as a serious matter of religious conduct. For in the last analysis, but rarely admitted, the tenets
of religious faith are seen to rest upon an illusion, useful for
ensuring social order and helpful for psychological comfort,
but hardly to be compared with the actual world of work.

This comparative lack of interest in doctrine and corresponding preoccupation with personal morality has colored
American thinking about religion, even by those altogether
opposed to religious belief. For example, beginning in 2008,
certain atheists sponsored an ad campaign featuring a (black)
man dressed in a Santa Claus suit with the caption, "Why
believe in a god? Just be good for goodness's sake."[35] What
is so interesting about these ads is that they did not offer
arguments against the existence of God or on behalf of the
self-subsistence of matter or anything of that sort whatsoever.

---

[35] Austen Ivereigh, "Atheist bus goes global," *America*, March 21, 2009,
https://www.americamagazine.org/content/all-things/atheist-bus-goes
-global.

They did not address the question of whether God exists at all. They simply exhorted one to be good without the help of God. They assumed, what Americans generally have assumed, that religion is first of all about morality, not about proclaiming or asserting truths, such as the Trinity or the incarnation or the resurrection of Our Lord. In taking the line they did, it would seem that the sponsors of the ads either shared in the general American understanding of religion or supposed that the vast majority of those who read the ads would do so.

And it seems they were right, judging from some of the responses by Protestant spokesmen to the ads. Os Guinness, a Protestant writer and social commentator, appeared to have the same understanding of the role of religion as did the atheists in his comments responding to the ads.

> "Yes, you can be good without God. There are many examples of that.
>
> "The real question is can you create a good society without God? The framers of the Constitution believed in religious liberty, for atheists too, but were leery of a whole society that was atheistic. Without God, you would not have virtue to restrain evil. Freedom requires order, and there is only one type of order compatible with freedom, self-restraint."
>
> In his Farewell Address as President, George Washington said, "Of all the dispositions and habits which lead to political prosperity, Religion and morality are indispensable supports. . . . And let us with caution indulge the supposition that morality can be maintained without religion."

> Guinness argues that "There has never been a major
> society that has been good and sustained its goodness
> without God. Atheistic societies have been profoundly
> evil and totalitarian."[36]

For Os Guinness, as for the atheists, the importance of religion appears to be not that it is or might be true but that it
is socially useful, if not absolutely necessary for an individual,
at least for society as a whole. This is not merely a downplay-
ing of doctrinal questions but an apparent utter disregard of
them. We might recall the apt words of C. S. Lewis in *The
Screwtape Letters* (letter 23): "Men or nations who think they
can revive the Faith in order to make a good society might
just as well think they can use the stairs of Heaven as a short
cut to the nearest chemist's shop."[37] I do not doubt, to be sure,
that Os Guinness sincerely believes in the doctrines of Evangelical Protestantism, but he easily falls into the trap of justi-
fying belief because of its presumed good effect on morality.

Guinness's citation of Washington's farewell address is very
interesting. Although frequently quoted by defenders of religion in American life, it seems that Washington's indifference
to the question of religious *truth* is not so frequently noted. It
is no doubt true that Washington more or less equated religion here with some form of Christianity, but still his recom-
mendation of religion was entirely based on its social benefits
and could be applied to any religion at all. While this might
be all that can be expected from a political figure, I do not

---

[36] www.virtueonline.org/portal/modular/news/article.php? storyid =95
25. This page does not appear to exist anymore on the Internet.
[37] C. S. Lewis, *The Srewtape Letters* (New York: Macmillan, 1961), 120.

understand how and why his words are quoted so confidently by religious figures who are representatives of various forms of Christian belief. Do they not see that the role Washington sets forth for religion could be applied regardless of the tenets of any particular religion? Do they equate social utility with truth, or is truth not important to them?

Washington's vision of religion seems akin to the proposal of the *noble lie* in Plato's *Republic*. This was a means suggested by Socrates as a way of making the citizens of the ideal city he and his friends were drawing up more devoted to their city and to one another by teaching them that the city's inhabitants literally grew from the city's soil. And thus, these citizens were in the closest sense brothers so that "as though the land they are in were a mother and nurse, they must plan for and defend it, if anyone attacks, and they must think of the other citizens as brothers and born of the earth."

It seems undeniable that even those who sincerely hold to some particular form of Christian doctrines tend to defend their religious beliefs on purely utilitarian grounds. It is seemingly natural for them to jump almost immediately from doctrine to morality, hardly realizing that they are making this leap.[38]

The question that faces us now is a historical one. How and why did "a new form of culture, and indeed a new type of Christianity, which was subsequently diffused all over

---

[38] Of course, it is natural to think that if any particular religion is true, then it also provides benefits both social and individual. To think this does not necessarily mean that the believer seeks to justify his beliefs exclusively or primarily by means of their moral or social effects in this world, but simply as a natural result of their truth.

the world, and especially in North America," come to be? We should recall that in discussing the American religious spirit, we are dealing with a Protestant religious spirit, one that broke away from the Catholic Church beginning in the sixteenth century. But as we saw above, the new religious doctrines created a new cultural world. That great historian of culture Christopher Dawson, whom I have already quoted more than once, describes the cultural development of Europe after the Protestant Reformation as the triumph of what he calls a bourgeois spirit or bourgeois civilization: "The conflict between these two ideals of life and forms of culture runs through the whole history of Europe from the Reformation to the Revolution and finds its political counterpart in the struggle between Spain and the Protestant powers. It is hardly too much to say that if Philip II had been victorious over the Dutch and the English and the Huguenots, modern bourgeois civilization would never have developed and capitalism in so far as it existed would have acquired an entirely different complexion."[39]

But this did not occur; rather the opposite. "In the lands where these [new, non-Catholic] ideals had free play— Holland, Great Britain, above all New England, a new type of character was produced, canny, methodical and laborious; men who lived not for enjoyment but for work, who spent little and gained much, and who looked on themselves as unfaithful stewards before God, if they neglected any opportunity of honest gain."[40]

---

[39] Dawson, "Catholicism and the Bourgeois Mind," in *Dynamics of World History*, 208.

[40] Christopher Dawson, "Economics in the Medieval and in the Modern

"Above all New England," wrote Dawson. Or as he says elsewhere, "In no country, save perhaps in the United States, does the bourgeois culture exist in the pure state as a self-subsistent whole."[41]

Lacking even the physical reminders of a past Catholic civilization that the countries of Europe have, and even more lacking any significant cultural or intellectual reminders of a Catholic past, we are easy prey for the charlatans who peddle the Prosperity Gospel. If Christianity is conceived as "focused on the subjective world of religious feeling—above all the intense experience of religious conversion," then there is little wonder that such a religion is divorced from both dogma and from any morality that goes beyond the level of individual conduct. Of course, it is true that all morality concerns the behavior of individuals. To drop bombs on civilians or to use economic pressure to lower wages or put competitors out of business are the actions of individual persons. But they are most often looked at as part of a larger and more impersonal and "objective world which was the domain of business and politics," and as a result, not really of any moral or especially religious concern.

Now we return full circle to the Joel Osteens, Paula Whites, and others. They are able to promote their distorted Gospel because Americans have been told for hundreds of years that the serious business of life is about making money, about getting ahead economically, and that everything else, when all is

---

World," *The Dawson Newsletter* 3, no. 4 (winter 1984-85): 3. (Reprinted from *Blackfriars*, July 1924.)

[41] Dawson, "Bolshevism and the Bourgeoisie," in *Dynamics of World History*, 229.

said and done, matters little or not at all. I quoted before from John Paul's encyclical *Centesimus Annus*, that "it is not possible to understand the human person on the basis of economics alone, nor to define the person simply on the basis of class membership. A human being is understood in a more complete way when situated within the sphere of culture through language, history, and the position one takes towards the fundamental events of life, such as birth, love, work and death."[42]

But this is not how we usually view things. Culture and language and history are irrelevancies to us. Ronald Reagan, in a speech on November 7, 1988, said, "I received a letter not long ago from a man who said, 'You can go to Japan to live, but you cannot become Japanese. You can go to France, and you'd live and not become a Frenchman. You can go to live in Germany or Turkey, and you won't become a German or a Turk.' But then he added, 'Anybody from any corner of the world can come to America to live and become an American.'"[43]

Reagan was correct in what he said. But is this for the good? Is this something to be celebrated? Does it highlight something admirable about this country? "A human being is understood in a more complete way when situated within the sphere of culture through language [and] history." Does not the fact that anyone can come to America and become an American indicate that for us, questions of culture, language, and history

---

[42] Pope John Paul II, *Centesimus Annus*, no. 24.
[43] Steven F. Hayward, "Ronald Reagan's Shining City of Exceptional Immigrants," *Forbes*, December 6, 2013, https://www.forbes.com/sites/stevenhayward/2013/12/06/ronald-reagans-shining-city-of-exceptional-immigrants/?sh=3cabfa68639ft. The same quote appears with slightly different wording elsewhere.

are not important? That becoming an American is something that can be understood largely on the basis of economics?

Earlier, I quoted the nineteenth-century Catholic politician Charles O'Connor that "in America, a man is accounted a failure, and ought to be, who has not risen above his father's station in life." If we accept this mandate, then what does this say about our feeling for *place*, for our own locality, for family even? Too often, to rise above one's father's station means to move away from where one grew up. To abandon one's family and friends, all in the name of worldly success and of increased income—does not this involve the comparative scorn for such values as culture, language, and history? Yes, there are some things money cannot buy, one of which is the happiness of living and dying by the people you love the most. And therefore, "It is not possible to understand the human person on the basis of economics alone"—but is this not what we do when we put economic advancement at the top of our wish list for our children—and for ourselves? Do we not proclaim, does our culture not proclaim, that economics is all we need to understand ourselves and one another?

Next, let us ask ourselves how it came about that, as Dawson put it, "in no country, save perhaps in the United States, does the bourgeois culture exist in the pure state as a self-subsistent whole."

For is it not the case that pretty much all of Europe has lost its Catholic culture, a demise that has been happening slowly or quickly since the French Revolution or even earlier? To consider this question fully we must look at how cultural traits continue or cease to exercise influence.

Let us begin with another quotation from Hilaire Belloc: "A nation like the French," he wrote, "may largely lose the doctrine of the Incarnation and of the Immortality of the soul . . . but even those who have lost the whole Catholic scheme of doctrine still continue the Catholic habit. They will continue the Catholic sense that justice is more important than order; the Catholic tendency to well-divided property; and the Catholic conviction of Free will."[44]

So a society's "morals, its intellectual habits, its strong traditions of behavior, all these proceed from the religious doctrines under which it has been formed," even when "those doctrines may have lost their original vitality."[45] Thus, the presence in southern Europe and Latin America, until recently at least, of a strong sense of family, including the extended family, is a cultural characteristic derived from Catholic Faith and morality. It long survived the fact that a vibrant Catholic doctrinal commitment was more and more weakening in those societies as a whole. That is why there are considerable differences between societies that can be termed post-Protestant from those that are post-Catholic. Each kind of society retains much from its theological past, even if each type has largely repudiated or forgotten the actual dogmas and doctrines which formed those societies.

The persistence of these cultural traits is one of the factors noted by Max Weber in his renowned book *The Protestant Ethic and the Spirit of Capitalism*. Weber, in many respects, laid the groundwork for comparing Protestants'

---

[44] Hilaire Belloc, "The Two Cultures of the West," in *Essays of a Catholic* (Rockford, IL: TAN Books, 1992), 240.
[45] Belloc, 240.

and Catholics' cultural approach to economic life. He noted, for example, that "among journeymen . . . the Catholics show a stronger propensity to remain in their crafts, that is they more often become master craftsmen, whereas the Protestants are attracted to a larger extent into the factories in order to fill the upper ranks of skilled labour and administrative positions. The explanation of these cases is undoubtedly that the mental and spiritual peculiarities acquired from the environment, here the type of education favoured by the religious atmosphere of the home community and the parental home, have determined the choice of occupation, and through it the professional career."[46]

We see here encapsulated the different attitudes toward work and moneymaking that lie at the heart of the two cultures. On the one hand, the desire to become a master of a craft—that is, to have a real connection with actual work and pride in that labor and with the actual economic process of fulfilling human needs by means of work; on the other hand, a preference for the administrative positions which are one step removed from the actual productive work of the firm and hence closer to the defining note of capitalism, the separation of ownership and work. But it is an ethic, a culture, which lies behind these choices. As Weber further declares:

> In fact, the *summum bonum* of this ethic, the earning
> of more and more money, combined with the strict

---

[46] Max Weber, *The Protestant Ethic and the Spirit of Capitalism* (New York: Charles Scribner's, 1958), 38–39.

avoidance of all spontaneous enjoyment of life, is above all completely devoid of any eudaemonistic, not to say hedonist, admixture. It is thought of so purely as an end in itself, that from the point of view of the happiness of, or utility to, the single individual, it appears entirely transcendental and absolutely irrational. Man is dominated by the making of money, by acquisition as the ultimate purpose of his life. Economic acquisition is no longer subordinated to man as the means for the satisfaction of his material needs. This reversal of what we should call the natural relationship, so irrational from a naive point of view, is evidently as definitely a leading principle of capitalism as it is foreign to all peoples not under capitalistic influence.[47]

Here we introduce a new note: the fact that capitalism's preoccupation with work and moneymaking is not always greed, *per se*, but something more than greed, in fact, a quasi-religious attitude. A late nineteenth-century German immigrant commented on his father-in-law.

"Couldn't the old man be satisfied with his $75,000 a year and rest? No! The frontage of the store must be widened to 400 feet. Why? That beats everything, he says. In the evening when his wife and daughter read together, he wants to go to bed. Sundays he looks at the clock every five minutes to see when the day will be over—what a futile life!" In these terms the son-in-law (who had emigrated from Germany) of

---

[47] Weber, 53.

the leading dry-goods man of an Ohio city expressed
his judgment of the latter, a judgment which would
undoubtedly have seemed simply incomprehensible to
the old man. A symptom of German lack of energy.[48]

The spirit of capitalism is something new in human affairs,
and it reverses the natural and hitherto dominant relationship between the worker and his work. Here we encounter
the notion of work and of moneymaking as an *ethical* imperative, expressing the attitude toward reality at the heart of
that culture, which had produced, as Christopher Dawson
noted, "a new type of character . . . , canny, methodical and
laborious; men who lived not for enjoyment but for work,
who spent little and gained much, and who looked on themselves as unfaithful stewards before God, if they neglected
any opportunity of honest gain."[49]

We may contrast this with the life which Weber calls the
"most important opponent with which the spirit of capitalism . . . has had to struggle" and which he says "we may
designate as traditionalism."[50] What did this "traditionalism"
comprise? There was the formal organization of a business
firm, but beyond that there was the spirit which animated
it: "The form of organization was in every respect capitalistic. . . . But it was traditionalistic business, if one considers
the spirit which animated the entrepreneur: the traditional
manner of life, the traditional rate of profit, the traditional
amount of work, the traditional manner of regulating the

---

[48] Weber, 283.
[49] Dawson, "Economics in the Medieval and in the Modern World," 3.
[50] Weber, *The Protestant Ethic and the Spirit of Capitalism*, 58–59.

relationships with labour, and the essentially traditional circle of customers and the manner of attracting new ones."[51]

Here we may see the essence of the matter. I previously quoted Fr. Anton Walburg's 1889 book *The Question of Nationality in its Relation to the Catholic Church*, that "the ideal set before every American youth is money. Money is not only needful, but is the one thing needful. Money is a power everywhere, but here it is the supreme power. . . . In Europe, a man enjoys his competence; but here, no one has enough."[52]

This desire for gain is not always simply an example of greed, or rather, not simply an example of pure greed. It possesses a religious meaning, albeit a perversion of the authentic Gospel of Jesus Christ, revealed most clearly in the Calvinism that dominated the colonial American religious landscape.

> The exhortation of the apostle to make fast one's own call is here interpreted as a duty to attain certainty of one's own election and justification in the daily struggle of life. In the place of the humble sinners to whom Luther promises grace if they trust themselves to God in penitent faith are bred those self-confident saints whom we can rediscover in the hard Puritan merchants of the heroic age of capitalism and in isolated instances down to the present. On the other hand, in order to attain that self-confidence intense worldly activity is recommended as the most suitable means.

---

[51] Weber, 67.

[52] Abell, *American Catholic Thought on Social Questions*, 40, 41, 43.

It and it alone disperses religious doubts and gives the certainty of grace.[53]

For, "labour came to be considered in itself the end of life, ordained as such by God."[54] Hence were produced "men who lived not for enjoyment but for work, who spent little and gained much, and who looked on themselves as unfaithful stewards before God, if they neglected any opportunity of honest gain," to quote Dawson once again. Thus Russell Conwell's advice, "I say that you ought to get rich, and it is your duty to get rich."[55] Your *duty*, note, or else we run the risk of being "unfaithful stewards before God."

An example of this disordered notion of work and leisure was the seventeenth-century English controversy between Puritans and Anglicans, who retained a measure of the old Catholic spirit. "As we have seen, this asceticism turned with all its force against one thing: the spontaneous enjoyment of life and all it had to offer. This is perhaps most characteristically brought out in the struggle over the *Book of Sports* which James I and Charles I made into a law expressly as a means of counteracting Puritanism, and which the latter ordered to be read from all the pulpits."[56]

---

[53] Weber, *The Protestant Ethic and the Spirit of Capitalism*, 111–12.

[54] Weber, 159.

[55] Russell H. Conwell, *Acres of Diamonds* (Project Gutenberg, 2008), https://www.gutenberg.org/files/368/368-h/368-h.htm.

[56] Weber, *The Protestant Ethic and the Spirit of Capitalism*, 166–67. The *Book of Sports* was a work commissioned by King James I to promote wholesome recreation on Sundays, contrary to the Puritans, who espoused an extreme Sabbatarianism which forbade such recreations.

This spirit manifested itself even in "the decline of lyric poetry and folk-music, as well as the drama, after the Elizabethan age in England."[57] All that remained then, was the pursuit of riches. "What the great religious epoch of the seventeenth century bequeathed to its utilitarian successor was, however, above all an amazingly good, we may even say a pharisaically good, conscience in the acquisition of money, so long as it took place legally."[58]

We see here two different conceptions of life, fueled, as Pope Saint John Paul II put it, by "the attitude a person takes to the greatest mystery: the mystery of God . . . different ways of facing the question of the meaning of personal existence."[59] The attitudes toward the Divine that different cultures possess manifest themselves in multiple ways, perhaps especially in their attitudes toward economics. We have seen some examples of how these are exhibited in Protestant cultures, particularly in that one culture in which Protestant attitudes have been most unopposed by any countervailing forces—that is, the culture of the United States. Our next task is to look at the specific ways that this Protestant culture has affected the various aspects of society.

---

[57] Weber, 272.
[58] Weber, 176.
[59] Pope John Paul II, *Centesimus Annus*, no. 24.

Chapter Two

Purpose and Freedom

In the previous chapter, we traced how Protestantism and its attitudes toward money and material things have impacted society and still impact Catholics who live within this Protestant milieu. We examined many specific examples of the immense social changes introduced by Protestantism and their effects on attitudes towards riches and material things and how this impacted and still impacts Catholics who live within this Protestant milieu. We also looked at some of the reasons for these changes. But before continuing with our examination of the effects of the new attitudes on various facets of society, we need to go to the very root of the matter. And this lies in modernity's loss of the sense that there is any inherent purpose in things, what philosophers call final causes.

One of the cardinal points in the philosophy of Aristotle and Saint Thomas is that everything acts for an end. Or, to put it in a slightly different way, we can say that everything exists for a purpose. Human beings, for example, are endowed with sexual organs fundamentally for the sake of the propagation of the species. We have the need and capacity to eat and drink in order to nourish ourselves and keep our bodies alive. If someone eats or drinks excessively and thereby harms his health, he is not only committing a sin of gluttony or drunkenness, not only harming his physical well-being, but he is acting against the very purpose for which eating and drinking primarily exist, which is the maintenance of our bodily health, not its impairment or destruction. Regardless of whether we recognize it or not, this is simply what eating and drinking are for. Of course, these have other legitimate ends—the pleasure of a good meal or a fine wine, the fellowship of dining together with family or friends. But these are subordinate ends in the sense that if these legitimate secondary ends hinder the primary end, especially if they hinder it in any serious way, we have subverted the inherent purpose for which we humans need food and drink.

But, by and large, modernity denies such truths and teaches that only our freely chosen ends or goals have any validity. There are no inherent purposes in things; ultimately, it is chance that has created the order we see in the cosmos. So there are no limits or restraints on what someone can think or do except the freely embraced limits which I acquiesce to and impose upon myself. For example, I may choose to obey the law and submit to the requirements of living in society in order to enjoy its benefits. One of the most explicit statements of this view was that written by Supreme Court justice Anthony Kennedy in his opinion in the 1992 case of *Planned Parenthood vs. Casey*: "At the heart of liberty is the right to define one's own concept of existence, of meaning, of the universe, and of the mystery of human life." Whether Justice Kennedy thought that one could actually *create* his own private universe is not clear, but what is clear is that Kennedy believed that each of us has the right to attempt to do so, unhampered not only by political or social restrictions but apparently by reality itself.

And behind all this lies the notion that the good is a matter of private choice, that, at least on the political level, no one has a right to tell anyone else that his own conception of God, of right and wrong, of social relations, of happiness or its pursuit is false. In short, each person has the right to his own conception "of existence, of meaning, of the universe, and of the mystery of human life."

It is obvious how similar this is to the Protestant principle according to which each person is free to read his Bible and decide for himself what it means, and hence, what he is permitted to do or not to do. Or, at best, only God Himself can speak to anyone and tell him he must do or not do something. But note that on this view, God speaks only to individuals. What you believe God is saying to you is your business alone, while I might think that He is saying something wholly different to me. Even though today only a minority of Americans read the Bible and listen to God in prayer, the secular version of this practice still thrives—that is, one's alleged right "to define one's own concept of existence, of meaning, of the universe, and of the mystery of human life."

The traditional view, however, held that human beings were bound to conform themselves and their actions to reality, a reality ultimately established by God. This reality includes the purposes inherent in actions and things, purposes beyond what we might freely choose for ourselves, and as a result, all the activities of our human nature, whether political, economic, educational, or whatever, have inherent ends which we are bound to conform ourselves to. No matter how much we might want to change the inherent purpose of human sexuality or of the human digestive process, we cannot do so. Purpose is built into the very structure of the universe as created by God. And in this structured universe, all human actions were not only connected but arranged in a hierarchy of means and ends, leading us ultimately to eternal life with God. But the entire modern project may be called one gigantic effort to deny that fact, to proclaim that there are no purposes except those an individual chooses for himself. Hence the subordinate aspects of human social life, such as the economy or artistic activity, have been loosed from their traditional place in the hierarchy of goods. There is now no hierarchy but simply a set of activities, each competing for our attention and seeking to dominate the other spheres of social life by seducing us or, in the worst case, simply by force.

Although what I am saying here applies to all aspects of human life, it is most obvious in the activities I have already mentioned, activities such as eating, drinking, or sexuality. The biological purpose of sex is clear: the conception of children. Moreover, it is obvious that unrestrained and unrestricted sexual activity does not provide well for the children who are the natural result of such activity. Hence every culture created various rules for safeguarding its children. Thus the universal or nearly universal institution of marriage throughout history, an institution surrounded by rites, laws, prohibitions, and so on which indicate that every culture, every society, realized its importance for the very survival of a people. Of course, marriage laws and customs differ, but amidst all of the variety, there is one constant: marriage exists for the propagation and nourishing of the young. Different societies, it is true, attempted to secure those ends in different ways, but each recognized the fact that unrestricted sexual activity would not safeguard the well-being of the next generation. Hence marriage and the family as more or less stable human institutions exist everywhere.

The modern view, however, is that sexuality and marriage have no inherent purpose apart from the subjective motives and desires of those seeking to enter into them. If freedom consists of our ability to construct or understand reality according to our own desires and vision, then we cannot condemn someone who thinks that marriage is simply a partnership for sexual fulfillment and companionship—in which case it would be difficult to deny that same-sex couples can get married. On such a view, we cannot assert, except as a purely subjective and personal opinion, that the primary or fundamental purpose of marriage is the procreation and education of children. Only if we recognize that marriage in reality does have an inherent purpose, regardless of anyone's personal "concept of existence," can we judge that marriage in fact has a meaning that is valid for everyone, no matter what one's own private views might be.

But if marriage does have such an inherent purpose, where does that purpose come from? From God, ultimately, the creator of everything. But it is vital to understand that this divinely-given purpose of marriage is not something imposed in an arbitrary manner upon an otherwise merely neutral activity. Marriage and sexuality have inherent purposes because those purposes are part of their very structure according to the way God created them. Just as we can say that the purpose of a particular tool, say a saw, is to cut simply because of the way that a saw is constructed. As long as it is a saw, that is its purpose. The designer or producer of a saw cannot simply give it any purpose of his choosing. Rather, it is the way that the saw is designed and made that gives it its purpose. Certainly, this is according to the intention of the designer, but the point is that by making an object with the characteristics of a saw, one automatically endows it with a certain purpose. The saw is for cutting because of the way it is.

With marriage and sexuality, this may be obvious, but it is not so obvious with regard to many of the other activities of human life, such as the state, economic activity, education, science, the arts, and so forth. They all have inherent purposes because of what they are. These purposes are neither arbitrary impositions by God nor free creations of each individual. We have no more right to ascribe our own purpose to marriage or to the economy or to education than we have to assert that a saw exists for the sake of drilling holes or hammering nails because that fits in better with any claimed "right to define one's own concept of existence, of meaning, of the universe, and of the mystery of human life." Just as saws have a definite shape and texture, definite characteristics that fit them for a particular task and no other, so do the various human activities and institutions I just enumerated.

The alternative to this view is the exaltation of the human will. Reality can become whatever I want it to be. This is nothing but the philosophy of Satan, who embraced the absurdity of considering himself God's equal. But it is nonsense. Satan is *not* God's equal. This is not an opinion, but a fact. Things do have definite natures, definite shapes and functions, and because of that, they have definite purposes. This applies not only to physical things but also, as I pointed out, to the processes and institutions of our social life. This would have been a commonplace to our ancestors, who saw created reality as not only having purpose but also having an intelligibility by which we can discern that purpose.

Moreover, it is important to realize that unless things have inherent purposes that we can recognize, it is impossible to make any kind of judgment about them. If something simply *is*, who is to say whether it is good or bad? It simply is. If I know that the purpose of a car is to get its driver and passengers safely and quickly from one point to another, then I can judge whether any particular car is good or not. But if it is simply a complicated mass of metal, plastic, and electronics, how can one say whether it is good or bad. Without recognition of purpose, nothing can be called good or evil, successful or unsuccessful. We recognize this fact implicitly when we judge the vast majority of things in this world, especially products of human art. We expect our cars to run efficiently, our furnaces to heat our houses reliably, our refrigerators to keep our food cool and fresh. Only when we turn to the more fundamental and more important questions of human existence are we apt to embrace the incoherent nonsense that one has a right "to define one's own concept of existence, of meaning, of the universe, and of the mystery of human life." But what is true of such humble objects as toasters or blenders is also true of "the mystery of human life." We do not create our own reality. Our task is to discover reality and conform ourselves to it. In the next few chapters, we will examine a range of human activities and institutions with a view toward discerning their inherent purposes, as well as the perversions of those purposes engaged in by the modern world.

CHAPTER THREE

Society and Politics

When we consider the implications of Justice Kennedy's affirmation of radical individualism contained in his dictum that "at the heart of liberty is the right to define one's own concept of existence, of meaning, of the universe, and of the mystery of human life," the very first social institution that we must look at is the state or political community. Why is this? It is because, as regards to life in this world, the political community is the basic human community, the community within which all our other actions take place. The German Thomistic philosopher, Josef Pieper, explained it in these words:

> The state, we may note, occupies a unique place in the scale that extends from the individual to the whole of mankind; more than anything else, it represents the "social whole." The idea of the common good is its distinctive attribute. A nation (in the midst of other nations) ordered in a state is the proper, historically concrete image of man's communal life. *Communitas politica est communitas principalissima*—Political community is community in the highest degree. In the fullest sense the state alone incorporates, realizes, and

administers the *bonum commune*. That does not mean, however, that the family, the community, free associations, and the Church are not important for the realization of the common good, too. But it means that the harmonizing and integration of nearly all men's functions occurs only in the political community.[60]

Aristotle had said the same thing centuries before, and his teaching was adopted and developed as part of the Church's own thought and philosophy. As Pope Leo XIII wrote,

Man's natural instinct moves him to live in civil society, for he cannot, if dwelling apart, provide himself with the necessary requirements of life, nor procure the means of developing his mental and moral faculties. Hence it is divinely ordained that he should lead his life—be it family, social, or civil—with his fellow men, among whom alone his several wants can be adequately supplied. But as no society can hold together unless some one be over all, directing all to strive earnestly for the common good; every civilized community must have a ruling authority, and this authority, no less than society itself, has its source in nature, and has, consequently, God for its author.[61]

This does not mean, of course, that the family exists as a creation of the political community or that it derives its purpose and rights from the political community. No, the family

---

[60] Josef Pieper, *The Four Cardinal Virtues* (Notre Dame: University of Notre Dame, 1966), 85.
[61] Pope Leo XIII, *Immortale Dei* (November 1, 1885), no. 3.

pre-exists the state, as Aristotle himself pointed out. But the entire tradition, from Aristotle to Leo XIII and beyond, also recognizes that the family by itself is not sufficient for man's complete welfare and development—that without "civil society . . . he cannot, . . . provide himself with the necessary requirements of life, nor procure the means of developing his mental and moral faculties." Just as an individual human person has a purpose and an integrity of his own not dependent upon any higher order, but nevertheless requires such a higher order for his own completion and perfection, so with the family. And just as the family has an inherent purpose, so political or civil society, as a natural institution, has a purpose of its own, one which we must recognize and conform ourselves to. We must now consider what this purpose is.

When thinking about the political community, Americans are apt to regard freedom as the chief political and social good that we possess, indeed as a principal end for which governments are established. And the kind of freedom which is meant is freedom from coercion on the part of the state. The ideal human condition, according to this view, lies in the notion that each individual is essentially independent from every other individual, in fact, in the supposed state of nature posited by some seventeenth- and eighteenth-century political philosophers. Government, then, has only a negative role: to protect each from encroachments on our rights and freedoms. As long as we refrain from infringing on other persons' rights by force or fraud, government is to stay out of our business. Something like this is widely held to be the essential note of genuine human freedom. According to this understanding, freedom is primarily about each person being able to do whatever he wants, unless that involves forceful or fraudulent actions toward another person. And for those who hold this view of freedom, it is chiefly the government which threatens our freedoms, and against whose intrusions, real or imagined, we must always be vigilant.

But this view of freedom in political matters implies a more fundamental conception of freedom, one which extends to every area of life and thought and is embodied, whether we realize it or not, in Justice Anthony Kennedy's aforementioned statement that "at the heart of liberty is the right to define one's own concept of existence, of meaning, of the universe, and of the mystery of human life." We have here the individual posited as the center not only of social or political life but also of one's deepest philosophical or religious ideas. Our conduct, our individual pursuit of happiness, is our affair alone, within the minimal framework of avoiding force or fraud. From this view follows the mistaken notion that my ideas of ultimate reality are simply *mine*, and since (so it is said) they won't hurt you or anyone else, they are no one else's business.

What follows from this? That society is simply a collection of individuals, each pursuing what he judges to be his good according to his own lights. Society and the political community exist essentially as an aggregation of separate persons who have come together in order to protect their pre-existing natural rights, including that of pursuing happiness according to each one's own judgment, in fact, of exercising the right "to define one's own concept of existence, of meaning, of the universe, and of the mystery of human life." Underlying this is the radical shift in attitudes from the traditional and medieval view, which saw ourselves as primarily parts of some community or other, and the modern view that we are primarily separate individuals. As put by Father Tomáš Petráček in his book *Church, Society and Change*, "On the theoretical level medieval culture nonetheless emphatically rejected the fulfillment of individual ambitions at the expense of the common good (*bonum commune*). . . . Without support in form of the family, kinship relations, local solidarities or guild or religious brotherhood the individual might perhaps survive, but his existence would be a wretched one. The medieval person was brought up in the view that there is a difference between justified pursuit of a just share in the running of society and its wealth and selfish self-promotion at the expense of the whole."[62]

It is difficult, perhaps nearly impossible, for a completely modern person to grasp what it felt like to see oneself as primarily and fundamentally not a separate individual, but a member of a family, an extended kinship group, or a guild or religious solidarity. The Church's social doctrine, nevertheless, has addressed this understanding of social existence directly. As Pope Saint John Paul II wrote in *Centesimus Annus*:

> In order to overcome today's widespread individualistic mentality, what is required is *a concrete commitment to solidarity and charity*, beginning in the family with the mutual support of husband and wife and the care which the different generations give to one another. . . .

---

[62] Tomáš Petráček, *Church, Society and Change* (Lublin: El-Press, 2014), 32.

Apart from the family, other intermediate communities exercise primary functions and give life to
specific networks of solidarity. These develop as real
communities of persons and strengthen the social
fabric, preventing society from becoming an anonymous and impersonal mass, as unfortunately often
happens today. It is in interrelationships on many lev-
els that a person lives, and that society becomes more
"personalized."[63]

The new view of society, which flows ultimately from the
Protestant doctrine of private interpretation of Scripture, and
tends toward seeing society as "an anonymous and impersonal mass," is deeply engrained in the American mind. The
entire social order, including especially government, then,
has merely a negative purpose—that is, to protect individual rights, including the right to hold fundamentally different ideas on the most important matters. Society is held
together simply on the basis of personal freedoms. But there
can be no cohesive society based merely on freedom, on each
person's liberty to create his own vision of reality. Eventually,
as we are seeing now, that leads only to chaos.

Is there another view of freedom that we can contrast with
this one? Pope Leo XIII's 1888 encyclical *Libertas* consists of a
comprehensive treatment of the subject of human liberty, focus-
ing on the real distinction between the classical and Catholic
understanding of freedom, on the one hand, and the modern
on the other. This distinction arises because the former understanding acknowledges a truth which the latter fails to recognize,

---

[63] Pope John Paul II, *Centesimus Annus* (May 1, 1991), no. 49.

nameley, that "the pursuit of what has a false appearance of good, though a proof of our freedom, just as a disease is a proof of our vitality, implies defect in human liberty. . . . God, although supremely free . . . nevertheless cannot choose evil; neither can the angels and saints, who enjoy the beatific vision."[64]

Our freedom of action in the political order, our freedom to order our thinking and acting according to our own conception "of the mystery of human life," is not the essence of freedom then. In fact, it turns out that freedom from political coercion is only one aspect of freedom and by no means the most fundamental. Pope Leo places freedom as the ability to choose the good, not in the exercise of the freedom of choice unrestrained by anything external. In other words, just as it is impossible for God to choose evil, even though He is supremely free, so similarly, political restraints can hinder us from choosing evil. However, these restraints are not true limitations on our genuine freedom since we can choose evil as much as we can choose good. "Therefore," Pope Leo continued, "the true liberty of human society does not consist in every man doing what he pleases, . . . but rather in this, that through the injunctions of the civil law all may more easily conform to the prescriptions of the eternal law."[65]

The notion that freedom from restraint on the part of government or any other authority pertains to the essence of freedom is a mistake. Freedom is essentially about using our intellect and will to choose the good.

---

[64] Pope Leo XIII, *Libertas* (June 20, 1888), no. 6.
[65] Pope Leo XIII, no. 10.

In chapter 1, I quoted Christopher Dawson that "every civilization . . . is the expression in social institutions and cultural activity of a faith or a vision of reality which gives the civilization its spiritual unity."[66] If this is correct, then, curiously enough, the seeming lack of a shared worldview for society that appears in Justice Kennedy's statement turns out in fact to be a worldview, which is itself based upon a central idea or shared "vision of reality." This central idea is nothing other than the privatizing of religion, in fact, the privatizing of meaning, a subject we have already considered.

But if the privatizing of religion turns out to be part of a common worldview, what follows from that? If each of us can create our own "vision of reality," does this not mean that there is nothing that is necessarily shared or common to all of us in this society? What did I mean by saying that in fact Justice Kennedy's dictum itself involves a worldview? The question answers itself, I think, when we carry these ideas to their logical conclusions. Only because the United States had a rough Protestant consensus, despite the legal prohibition of any governmental religious establishment, has it held together as a society. Although obviously a Catholic would find much to criticize in that consensus, it remains a fact that without religion, American society would not have endured. When Catholic immigrants became Americanized, they became Protestantized, not of course necessarily with regard to their purely dogmatic beliefs, but with regard to those moral and cultural and political ideas that affected their conduct in American

---

[66] Christopher Dawson, *Understanding Europe* (Garden City, NY: Image, 1960), 211.

society. Whether one believes in the immaculate conception of the Blessed Virgin or not, or whether one holds that there is such a thing as purgatory, need not affect how one behaves in the world of business or politics. This philosophy of freedom, whether describing the political order or the entire range of our deepest metaphysical and theological attitudes, underlies the attitudes that modernity takes with regard to all or nearly all of the institutions and activities of our daily lives.

Thus the worldview that masquerades behind the assertion of absolute freedom to create one's own reality turns out to be the primacy of "the objective world which was the domain of business and politics," as Christopher Dawson expressed it.[67] We see, then, that the assertion of a pretty much unlimited freedom to shape reality to one's own wishes, as found in Justice Kennedy's statement, is in fact meaningless. Why? Because the subjective world that each of us can create has no effect on the real business of living, on the political or commercial activities out of which our life is constructed and which, according to this view, are the only really real things that there are. In other words, what is important in life is the material world which involves "business and politics," and to which religion is alien, "so that, as several Americans have remarked to me, they find some difficulty in relating the two concepts of religion and civilization since these seem to belong to two quite distinct orders of existence."[68] And while explicit considerations of ultimate meaning, of what John Paul called "the greatest mystery:

---

[67] Christopher Dawson, "America and the Secularization of Modern Culture," a lecture delivered at the University of Saint Thomas, Houston, Texas, 1960.
[68] Dawson, "America and the Secularization of Modern Culture."

the mystery of God," are merely private opinions, society overall pronounces very clearly on them: the real business of living
concerns such matters as business and politics. Anything else
is simply froth, ultimately of little or no importance. Justice
Kennedy's seemingly generous permission to create one's own
reality turns out to have a catch to it: the reality or meaning
you create for yourself hardly matters for the real business of
living. For the matters with which the domain of business and
politics is concerned are real enough: money and power. There
is nothing subjective about them, and when we consign "the
right to define one's own concept of existence, of meaning, of
the universe, and of the mystery of human life" to the purely
private and subjective sphere, nothing is left but the pursuit of
the obvious facts of wealth and power.

This merely private role for religion and the accompanying notion that our common life should concern itself solely
with external, tangible things, is directly based on the political philosophy of John Locke, and as formalized in the First
Amendment to the Constitution, it removes religion—and
hence any collective concern with ultimate questions—from
being a concern of society as a whole. In Locke's political
philosophy, men unite into society for one chief reason: "The
great and chief end, therefore, of men uniting into com-
monwealths, and putting themselves under government, is
the preservation of their property; to which in the state of
Nature there are many things wanting."[69]

---

[69] *Concering Civil Government, Second Essay*, in *Locke, Berkeley, Hume, Great Books of the Western World*, vol. 35 (Chicago: Encyclopaedia Britannica, 1952), 53. We may note here that Locke uses the term *property* as
a shorthand for "lives, liberties and estates, which I call by the general name
- property" (no. 123).

Or as he says elsewhere,

> The commonwealth seems to me to be a society of men constituted only for the procuring, preserving, and advancing their own civil interests.
>
> Civil interests I call life, liberty, health, and indolency of body; and the possession of outward things, such as money, lands, houses, furniture, and the like.[70]

The state and society as a whole have no concern for religious matters, nor with morality, beyond what is necessary to the preservation of public peace. Questions of ultimate meaning reside with the individual. As Locke further posits, "If a heathen doubt of both Testaments, he is not therefore to be punished as a pernicious citizen. The power of the magistrate and the estates of the people may be equally secure whether any man believe these things or no. . . . [For] the business of laws is not to provide for the truth of opinions, but for the safety and security of the commonwealth and of every particular man's goods and person."[71]

Locke's statement is a less comprehensive way of saying what Anthony Kennedy wrote over two centuries later. For just as it is of no concern to Locke what an unbeliever thinks about the deepest matters, so long as he does not threaten my property, so Justice Kennedy concedes the right to believe whatever anyone should wish, with the implied proviso, of course, that all such persons must obey

---

[70] John Locke, *A Letter Concerning Toleration*, in *Locke, Berkeley, Hume, Great Books of the Western World*, vol. 35, (Chicago: Encyclopedia Britannica, 1952), 3.

[71] Locke, 15.

the laws. For just as Locke thought that a "heathen [who doubts] of both Testaments" will not necessarily threaten anyone's liberty or property, so the most outlandish ideas "of existence, of meaning, of the universe, and of the mystery of human life" that someone holds will likewise not disturb society, so long as he observes laws respecting property and individual rights.

But this is not what Catholic doctrine and tradition have taught about the social order. For the Catholic tradition has always insisted that questions of meaning—that is, ultimately questions of religion—concern not merely individuals but the community as a whole, for the kingship of Jesus Christ extends to society and even the political order. In his encyclical *Quas Primas*, Pope Pius XI declares, "The empire of our Redeemer embraces all men. . . . Nor is there any difference in this matter between the individual and the family or the State; for all men, whether collectively or individually, are under the dominion of Christ. In him is the salvation of the individual, in him is the salvation of society."[72]

Society, including a political community, is not merely a collection of individuals; it, like the individual or the family, is part of the order established by God and exists for a purpose. Centuries before Pius XI, Saint Thomas Aquinas, in his *De Regimine Principum*, wrote, "It seems moreover to be the purpose of the multitude joined together to live according to virtue. . . . The virtuous life therefore is the purpose of the human community." He even adds that "the ultimate end of

---

[72] Pope Pius XI, *Quas Primas* (December 11, 1925), no. 18.

the multitude joined together is not to live according to virtue, but through virtuous living to attain to enjoyment of God."

But if this is true, if society or even the political community is to be about more than protection of property and individual rights, then it follows that the community as such must have some concern with both religion and morality. Otherwise, we are left with Justice Kennedy's relativism, his idea that freedom entails "the right to define one's own concept of existence, of meaning, of the universe, and of the mystery of human life." In the late nineteenth century, Pope Leo XIII carefully restated Catholic teaching on these important questions about the social order. His teaching can be summed up in this passage from his encyclical *Immortale Dei*:

> Nature and reason, which command every individual devoutly to worship God in holiness, because we belong to Him and must return to Him, since from Him we came, bind also the civil community by a like law. For, men, living together in society are under the power of God no less than individuals are, and society, no less than individuals, owes gratitude to God who gave it being and maintains it and whose ever-bounteous goodness enriches it with countless blessings. Since, then, no one is allowed to be remiss in the service due to God, and since the chief duty of all men is to cling to religion in both its teaching and practice— not such religion as they may have a preference for, but the religion which God enjoins, and which certain and most clear marks show to be the only one true

religion—it is a public crime to act as though there were no God . . . or out of many forms of religion to adopt that one which chimes in with the fancy; for we are bound absolutely to worship God in that way which He has shown to be His will.[73]

But the duty to worship God individually and corporately cannot exist if the state is prohibited from having any official or semi-official opinions on religious questions, which are relegated to the private realm, since each person's individual opinions about ultimate matters, matters of meaning, religion, and morality, are considered as equally valid in the eyes of the community, because the community as such has no opinions on such matters nor has any right to such an opinion.

Although originally Protestants were as concerned as were Catholics with the religious unity of their countries, there is a dissipating principle in Protestantism, based on the presumed right of private judgment, that eventually asserted itself. If everyone is free to interpret Scripture himself, and if society will not hold together if everyone is seeking to impose his interpretation on everyone else, the obvious solution is to remove religion from the public square and restrict it to the private realm. This neutralizes religion as a real force in society. It is now merely a private source of spiritual solace or psychological support, but not something to be taken seriously in "the objective world which was the domain of business and politics," as Dawson put it. Just as the Protestant principle rejects the idea that an ecclesiastical

---

[73] Pope Leo XIII, *Immortale Dei* (November 1, 1885), no. 6.

hierarchy can dictate to an individual believer in matters of faith or morals, so in the political or social realm, there is no earthly ruler or governing power who has any authority over the community in regard to its deepest beliefs.

John Locke's political philosophy, then, is simply a way of interjecting the Protestant principle of private judgment into the political and social realm in a supposedly religiously neutral manner—that is, without the need of an appeal to Scripture or to any explicit theological idea whatsoever. But Locke simply assumes that ideas about the most important matters are necessarily so private that no community, either formally or informally, has anything to say about them. The line from Protestant private judgment to John Locke to Anthony Kennedy can be traced with no difficulty.

Now it might seem that this is exactly as it should be. Why should civil rulers, who are apt to be mistaken about many things, have any authority in matters of ultimate beliefs? And when the question is posed in this way, I would not disagree. But this is an erroneous way of stating the question. It is not a matter of the imposition by governments of theological or philosophical principles versus our rights in conscience, but rather a matter of whether theological or philosophical ideas have any rightful presence at the societal level or whether they are purely private, and hence ultimately irrelevant to the real business of living, which turns out to be the acquisition and preservation of worldly goods.

The Protestant principle of private interpretation of Scripture, along with John Locke's political philosophy, ultimately based on his metaphysics, understand human life and institutions as devoid of any inherent purpose, except such purposes as each individual chooses to create for himself.[74] But here again we encounter a contrast with the philosophy of the Church, a contrast between the philosophy of nature and the metaphysics of classical and Catholic philosophy.

Since the understanding of truth and of society contained in the dictums of Locke and Anthony Kennedy relegates questions of ultimate meaning to the private realm, what does this imply for the theoretical underpinnings of the social order? If we are left with only the pursuit of power and riches, then whence does political authority derive its legitimacy? Not from God or from the nature of reality, since these have become simply matters of private opinion. There is nothing left now except the will to power, and it is upon this that political power must rest. The result, doubtless not obvious to either John Locke or Anthony Kennedy, is simply tyranny, at least potentially: the tyranny of a regime that imposes itself by force and by no inherent right nor according to the God-given purposes of things. For either a ruling power, in Church or state, receives its authority from God according to its own nature or it seizes it purely by force. In other words, the only alternative to legitimate authority, ultimately grounded in God and the order of creation, if we are to avoid the chaos of opposing opinions, is simply force. If political power is necessary for stable human living, then that power either exists by divine and natural right or it must assert its authority merely by means of its power. As John Paul II wrote in *Centesimus Annus*, "If one does not acknowledge

---

[74] This necessarily follows from Locke's nominalism. See, for example, his *Essay Concerning Human Understanding*, book 3, chapter 3, no. 11.

transcendent truth, then the force of power takes over, and each person tends to make full use of the means at his disposal in order to impose his own interests or his own opinion, with no regard for the rights of others."[75]

This tyranny, so far at least, has remained mostly hidden, latent, waiting in the wings. But it is there, if and when it is needed. In the meantime, we are told that we are free to conduct our lives according to Justice Kennedy's dictum, that each person can create his "own concept of existence, of meaning, of the universe, and of the mystery of human life," while in fact wealth and the will to power are the controlling principles. Unfortunately, these erroneous beliefs have had widespread consequences on humanity. In the next several chapters, we will look in more detail at the varying subordinate departments of human social life and consider the place that they occupy—or should occupy—according to their own nature as God has established them.

---

[75] Pope John Paul II, *Centesimus Annus*, no. 44.

CHAPTER FOUR

The Economic Order

Economic activity is one of the most important aspects of human life. Although Marxism incorrectly sees economic activity as *the* ruling element in man's social life, ascribing to it the role of creating and shaping the remainder of our cultural life—which it terms the "superstructure"— nevertheless economic activity can and often does have much weight in shaping the course of history. If a famine or plague should destroy a nation's capacity to feed itself, for example, then either extinction or mass emigration must follow. But despite its importance, the economy is not *the* key element in our social life. In fact, it reflects the more fundamental cultural attitudes at which we have already looked in this book, and it exists, or ought to exist, as part of the hierarchy of human activities. And when economic life is no longer seen and treated as an important but subordinate aspect of man's life, then it tends to take over and distort our social and moral values and alter our perceptions of the good. Pope Pius XI spoke explicitly to this point in these words:

> For it is the moral law alone which commands us to seek in all our conduct our supreme and final end, and to strive directly in our specific actions for those

ends which nature, or rather, the Author of Nature, has established for them, duly subordinating the particular to the general. If this law be faithfully obeyed, the result will be that particular economic aims, whether of society as a body or of individuals, will be intimately linked with the universal teleological order, and as a consequence we shall be led by progressive stages to the final end of all, God Himself, our highest and lasting good.[76]

Like any other of the subordinate factors of human life, the economy assumes its true worth only when it is firmly placed within the entire hierarchy of human social life, and if it escapes from that hierarchy, then it distorts not only society but also its own proper nature and purpose as well. In this chapter, we will examine the true place and value of economic activity and look at some of the customs, rules, and institutions erected by Christian civilization to keep it within its proper place in the hierarchy of man's activities and values.

We began this book by looking at some of the grotesque manifestations of the unfettered desire for money that have been remarked on so often as one of the more obvious distortions of American civilization. We have seen the contrast between this desire for riches and the teachings of Sacred Scripture. Before examining medieval Christendom's practices and the Church's more recent social teachings, we must look at the proper role which economic activity should play in society.

---

[76] Pope Pius XI, *Quadragesimo Anno* (May 15, 1931), no. 43.

God has created the human race so that we need to engage in economic activity in order to survive. Except in a few exceptional places where people might obtain sufficient food from a bountiful earth, we generally need to engage in agriculture, hunting, or fishing in order to obtain the nourishment we need. Besides food and drink, our lives would be poor and weak without clothing, shelter, or medicine. And although we do not absolutely require the remaining products of the arts and technology, they enhance our existence, making it more properly human and raising it above the level of mere survival.

But just as too much food or drink can harm us and are obvious perversions of the right use of those items, so we can misuse external goods. For example, we all need a dwelling place, and some people might need more than one, but at some point, the accumulation of dwellings ceases to make sense. They serve no rational purpose. No one could spend an appreciable amount of time in all those houses, and the mere ownership of them would violate the reason that human beings need shelter and private property. They would no longer protect us from the elements but rather sit empty most of the year. Or if I have so much miscellaneous stuff that I have to rent storage units to keep it all, then most likely I have too much stuff. I am not using it in accordance with its purpose; it is not serving the function for which it exists. External goods, property of all types, then, have an inherent purpose as much as food or drink, and to possess more than we reasonably need is to misuse such goods. We *can* have too much, either of goods or of money, and aside from endangering our eternal salvation, we are perverting the natural or inherent purposes of material goods.

Saint Thomas Aquinas pointed out that "the appetite of natural riches is not infinite, because according to a set measure they satisfy nature."[77] Our natural need for nourishment or shelter or anything else has inherent limits, the limits established by nature and thus by God in creating us the way that He did. We can only eat so much in one day and cannot live in more than one house at a time. If we insist on having more than we need, then we are perverting the inherent ends of these things.

But Saint Thomas also immediately went on to say that "the appetite of artificial riches is infinite, because it serves inordinate concupiscence." Artificial riches—money or stock certificates, for example—do not take up much room in our houses. It is probably obvious to most people that it is irrational to accumulate too much physical stuff. But it is not so clear with regard to "artificial riches." But if we consider that such "artificial riches" are mere surrogates for actual physical things, then we can see that likewise there is a natural limit on how much we can rationally possess. It is not irrational to want to save to provide against future emergencies or future events that are certain to come, such as old age, and while it may be difficult to state exactly what is a just amount of savings, surely at some point we can say we have enough, we don't honestly need any more. Anything else is simply "inordinate concupiscence."

---

[77] Thomas Aquinas, *Summa Theologiae* (Westminster MD: Christian Classics, 1981), I-II, q. 2, a. 1, ad 3.

If this is the correct attitude toward material riches, what has the Church and Catholic civilization done to make such an attitude part of our life? How was that attitude embodied in the civilization of the Middle Ages, and how have the popes in their modern social teaching attempted to continue that teaching? For both the Christian society of the Middle Ages and Catholic social teaching of the last century and a half, as a response on the part of the Church to the radically changed social conditions of modernity, presuppose that economic activity, like all of human life, has an intrinsic purpose, part of the very nature of that activity as something arising out of how God has created us.

Before looking at this, however, it would be well to confront a major difficulty. This is the fact that very many Catholics in the United States, and often those who proclaim most vehemently their adherence to the Church's magisterial teaching, explain away or even outrightly reject the Church's social doctrine as that has been reiterated again and again in the modern era. The questioning or rejection of the Church's advocacy of a living wage, of limitations on free competition in the marketplace, of the necessary role of labor unions, in fact, of a conception of the economy very unlike what most Americans are accustomed to hold, too often can lead to what in fact is dissent from Catholic teaching, very like the dissent of Catholics who favor the ordination of women or contraception. But in this case, the dissenting Catholics have convinced themselves that they are not really dissenters. What are the reasons for this? The background for this is complicated and well worth looking at. In the 1930s and '40s and even beyond, it was normal for instructed Catholics to judge American society, and especially the American economy, according to the prescriptions of the Church's social doctrine. Popular preachers such as Fulton Sheen could say over the radio in 1938 that "the Church is clearly and undeniably opposed to Capitalism."[78] But obviously this is not the case today. How did this enormous change come about?

Before the Second Vatican Council and its subsequent sweeping changes, Catholics in this country formed a much more self-conscious subculture. As a group, Catholics, especially educated Catholics, had a more cohesive Catholic identity and loyalty to the Church and her teachings than is usually the case today. Although, as we have seen, the Catholic mind was corrupted by the American Protestant milieu well before the 1960s, still there was more of a sense of Catholic solidarity, of a recognition that we were in important ways different from American Protestant society, and consequently, there was a greater tendency to recognize and accept what the Church actually taught. There existed what we may call a Catholic *tribe*, a subculture that embodied and protected Catholic life. However, this Catholic ethos was altered following the Second Vatican Council and, in part, as a response to changes in the larger American Society.

Because of the rapid and immense changes in the life of the Church that occurred in the five years after the council ended in 1965, many Catholics were disoriented, and understandably

---

[78] Fulton Sheen, *Justice & Charity* (American Chesterton Society, 2016), 28. Monsignor Sheen means here by capitalism not the private ownership of property but the amassing of property in the hands of the rich and the subsequent exploitation of the worker. He is quite clear about the social duties of property.

so. Although nothing essential in the Church's constitution and life changed, the ordinary Catholic of the time can be forgiven for thinking that it was no longer the same Church. Add to that the fact that prominent clerics and theologians could proclaim ideas clearly at variance with Catholic teaching and only rarely did bishops or religious superiors seem to care enough to attempt to silence such dissent, while the secular media was only too happy to promote these dissenters as the future of the Catholic Church. This confusion weakened the attachment of Catholics to the Church, and even alienated them from the shepherds who were supposed to be their spiritual guardians, but who seemed more concerned about not shaking up the status quo too much.

Then, at the same time, gigantic changes were occurring in society at large. Opinions that previously were unthinkable or advocated only by a small minority now began to be embraced by important segments of the ruling cultural and political class. Roughly before 1970, most Catholics were adherents of the Democratic Party, the party that had been friendliest to our immigrant ancestors and whose economic program, by and large, accorded reasonably well with the Church's own socio-economic teachings. Catholics in fact were an important part of the Democratic coalition and probably the largest component of the related labor movement. But as other elements in that coalition began to embrace causes such as abortion, the Equal Rights Amendment, and eventually the agenda of the homosexual movement, the Democratic Party leadership showed how much they valued the opinions of Catholic voters by totally embracing these new ideas.

By at least the late '80s, the Democrats' attitude seemed to be, Catholics be damned. Unless a Catholic Democrat was willing to defy the Church on these issues, increasingly he was no longer a valued member of what had been the New Deal coalition. Not surprisingly, this drove many Catholics into the Republican Party, and large numbers of them began to adopt the pro-business, *laissez-faire* philosophy of the Republicans, even though it stood in strong contrast to what the Church herself taught and to the historic position of most Catholics in the United States. As a result, many Catholics have become accustomed to regarding any attack on free-market capitalism as necessarily coming from their enemies, socialists or communists probably, since they assume that only they can have anything bad to say about our economic system.

Over time, a very powerful network of media outlets, educational institutions, and other organizations has arisen, largely funded by those who stand to profit by Republican economic policies, and whose aim is to convince Catholics that faithful and orthodox believers must adhere across the board to what in the United States is called a *conservative* political stance, although in fact, it mostly represents the classical liberalism of the eighteenth and nineteenth centuries. Right now, the hegemony of this network is almost impossible to challenge effectively.

This being the case, it is often hard to get a hearing for the social doctrine of the Church today. Yet this doctrine is an integral part of the Faith of the Church, as can be shown by numerous papal statements. In one of the strongest, Pope Pius XI, in his encyclical *Ubi Arcano* (1922), condemned those who downplay or belittle social doctrine, and went so far as to say, "In all this we recognize a kind of moral, judicial, and social Modernism, and We condemn it as strongly as We do dogmatic Modernism."[79] In fact, as John Paul II wrote in his 1987 encyclical *Sollicitudo Rei Socialis*, "The teaching and spreading of her social doctrine are part of the Church's evangelizing mission."[80] There is no escaping from this repeated teaching of the Church.

The Church's modern social doctrine was developed in response to the unprecedented cultural, social, economic, and technological changes that occurred in Europe starting in the sixteenth century, but which gained both speed and force with the technological developments of the eighteenth and nineteenth centuries. Before then, mankind's economic and even social life had rested mainly on a foundation of agriculture. While there had been technological improvements during that time, they were comparatively rare and in general did not unduly disturb the rhythm of economic or social life. Slavery had gradually withered away in response to the subtle effect of Catholic teaching, but again this shift from bondman to free peasant did not fundamentally disturb European life. The Church's economic ethic found little to criticize in either the feudal system (as that was moderating itself over the course of the Middle Ages) or still less in the urban economies, dominated as they were by those quintessentially Catholic institutions, the craft guilds. The Church did repeatedly clash with the increasingly important

---

[79] Pope Pius XI, *Ubi Arcano* (December 23, 1922), no. 61.

[80] Pope John Paul II, *Sollicitudo Rei Socialis* (December 30, 1987), no. 41.

banking and commercial sectors over the question of usury, and the fact that the Church continued to uphold the injustice of usury in the face of the nascent capitalist economy shows that the later elaboration of her social doctrine was no novelty but a necessary part of her critique of society.

Pope Pius XI, in his remarkable 1931 encyclical *Quadragesimo Anno*, summed up the Church's view on this long-vanished medieval socio-economic order:

> At one period there existed a social order which, though by no means perfect in every respect, corresponded nevertheless in a certain measure to right reason according to the needs and conditions of the times. That this order has long since perished is not due to the fact that it was incapable of development and adaptation to changing needs and circumstances, but rather to the wrong-doing of men. Men were hardened in excessive self-love and refused to extend that order, as was their duty, to the increasing numbers of the people; or else, deceived by the attractions of false liberty and other errors, they grew impatient of every restraint and endeavored to throw off all authority.[81]

The medieval mind recognized that one of the effects of the fall of our first parents was a tendency toward inordinate attachment to material goods and to money, the universal means by which to obtain such goods. What did the medieval Church do to counteract this sinful tendency of fallen mankind?

---

[81] Pope Pius XI, *Quadragesimo Anno*, no. 97.

The Church in medieval times did not hesitate to formulate a social moral code. It had specific teachings on the purpose of man's life and the place of material things in this over-all picture. The doctrine of justice was applied in detail to the market place. While the institution of private property was upheld, the social obligations of ownership were also stressed. The prime importance of the common welfare, as contrasted with individual selfish aims, was insisted upon. . . .

In the Christian society of the Middle Ages, the teaching of theologians and the sermons of preachers were more than mere exhortations. They laid down binding rules of conduct, accepted as moral obligations upon the consciences of individual Christians.[82]

Worthy of mention here was the Church's robust teaching on the immorality of usury; that is, if a lender demanded from a creditor more than the face value of a loan, *simply by virtue of the fact that it was a loan*, this was simply usury and hence unjust, regardless of the rate of interest demanded or the purpose of the loan. It was recognized that there were times when it was just to take interest on a loan, but only in special circumstances, such as when a lender would suffer harm because he did not have access to his funds for the period of the loan. The subject is complex and generated a huge debate among moral theologians and canonists from the High Middle Ages until the eighteenth century. But the Church's insistence on upholding her teachings about justice

---

[82] John F. Cronin, *Catholic Social Principles* (Milwaukee: Bruce, 1950), 11–12.

in the marketplace shows clearly her concern that economic activity be conducted within the bounds of both commutative and distributive justice.

To a Catholic of the Middle Ages, all such truths were obvious, and people were reminded of them again and again in sermons, tracts, and popular religious drama. They created a type of society which, as a matter of policy, attempted to keep riches and the acquiring of riches within their place as subsidiary human activities, important obviously, but all too likely to entangle our souls in sinful desires that, if unchecked, could lead to eternal damnation.

The English economic historian Richard Tawney conveys some idea of the contents of the medieval conception of the purpose of material goods: "Material riches are necessary; they have a secondary importance, since without them men cannot support themselves and help one another; the wise ruler, as St. Thomas said, will consider in founding his State the natural resources of the country. But economic motives are suspect. Because they are powerful appetites, men fear them, but they are not mean enough to applaud them. Like other strong passions, what they need, it is thought, is not a clear field, but repression. There is no place in medieval theory for economic activity which is not related to a moral end."[83]

Tawney continues with his description of medieval economic ethics:

---

[83] Richard H. Tawney, *Religion and the Rise of Capitalism* (New York: Harcourt, Brace, 1926), 31–32.

At every turn, therefore, there are limits, restrictions, warnings, against allowing economic interests to interfere with serious affairs. It is right for a man to seek such wealth as is necessary for a livelihood in his station. To seek more is not enterprise, but avarice, and avarice is a deadly sin. Trade is legitimate; the different resources of different countries show that it was intended by Providence. But it is a dangerous business. A man must be sure that he carries it on for the public benefit, and that the profits which he takes are no more than the wages of his labor.[84]

As another writer, Dominican Father Bede Jarrett, put it, "We can, therefore, lay down as the first principle of mediaeval economics that there was a limit to money-making imposed by the purpose for which the money was made. Each worker had to keep in front of himself the aim of his life and consider the acquiring of money as a means only to an end, which at one and the same time justified and limited him. When, therefore, sufficiency had been obtained there could be no reason for continuing further efforts at getting rich, . . . except in order to help others."[85]

In the phrase "there was a limit to money-making imposed by the purpose for which the money was made," we can discern the key to understanding the medieval mind, indeed, the Catholic mind. Life on this earth is oriented toward one supreme goal: our eternal life with God. While it is true that

---

[84] Tawney, 31–32.
[85] Bede Jarrett, *Social Theories of the Middle Ages* (Westminster, MD: Newman, 1942), 157–58.

not everything we do here below need be directly ordered toward that goal, anything that makes that goal harder to attain or, still more, that conflicts with that goal is dangerous or sinful. Too often we forget that avarice or greed is one of the seven deadly sins. And therefore, it is one of the least likely confessed sins. Another Dominican, Venerable Louis of Granada, who lived at the end of the Middle Ages, offers this powerful spiritual reminder of wealth's fleeting allure in the face of death:

> Death will rob you of all your earthly possessions; your works, good and bad, will alone accompany you beyond the tomb. If this dread hour finds you unprepared, great will be your misfortune. All that remains to you will then be distributed into three portions: Your body will become the food of worms; your soul the victim of demons; and your wealth the prey of eager and perhaps ungrateful or extravagant heirs. Ah! Dear Christian, follow the counsel of Our Savior; share your wealth with the poor, that it may be borne before you into the kingdom which you hope to enjoy. What folly to leave your treasures in a place of banishment whither you will never return, instead of sending them before you to that country which is intended for your eternal home![86]

And Venerable Louis of Granada further wrote, "Therefore, you rob the poor whenever you refuse to succor them from

---

[86] Louis of Granada, *The Sinner's Guide* (Charlotte, NC: TAN Books, 2014), 313.

your abundance. The riches you have received from God are meant to remedy human misery, not to be the instruments of a bad life. Therefore, do not let your prosperity cause you to forget the Author of all your blessings, and let not those blessings be a subject of vainglory. Do not, I conjure you, prefer a land of exile to your true country."[87]

Of course it is the case that in the Middle Ages, there were greedy men too. But the medievals faced up to two things that we too often fail to: that greed could be a deadly sin and that in order to avoid that sin, it was necessary to create concrete practices, institutions, and regulations which restrained greed. Just as orthodox Catholics of our day recognize that the strong human sexual drive must be guided and restrained in order for it to keep to the channels of virtue, our medieval ancestors saw that the same thing was true with regard to the desire for riches.

In addition to sermons, tracts, and popular dramas that exposed the dangers of greed, the medievals realized that there was a need for concrete regulations and, more importantly, institutions which could place a check on human avarice. In the medieval urban economy, most of those regulations centered around one of the most interesting of institutions: the craft guilds.

> A guild was a federation of autonomous workshops, whose owners (the masters) normally made all decisions and established the requirements for promotion from the lower ranks (journeymen or hired helpers, and apprentices). Inner conflicts were usually

---

[87] Louis of Granada, 314.

minimized by a common interest in the welfare of the craft and a virtual certitude that sooner or later every proficient apprentice and industrious journeyman would become a master and share in the governance of the craft. To make sure that expectations would be fulfilled, a guild would normally forbid overtime work after dark and sometimes limit the number of dependents a master could employ; this also served to maintain substantial equality among masters and to prevent overexpansion of the craft.[88]

How, in fact, did these guilds operate, and what were the rules which they made for their members? The statutes of the bakers' guild of Exeter provided that the guild wardens "have full power to examine, along with one of the officers of the city," the shops of individual bakers, looking for defects in flour or other items.[89] The Bristol fullers arranged to have "four men of the craft . . . chosen as Masters" who would "search every house of the said craft, twice a-week, and oversee all defects in the said cloths, if any there be."[90] In both cases, if any defect was found, a fine was payable, half to the guild and half to the city government.

---

[88] Robert S. Lopez, *The Commercial Revolution of the Middle Ages, 950-1350* (Cambridge: Cambridge University Press, 1976), 127.

[89] They "haffe fulle powere to make serche, with one of the officeris of the cite, as well vppon thoo that byeth mele contrary to the custume of the cite, as vppon gode paste to be made acordynd to the sise, as vppon all oder defavtys". [Joshua] Toulmin Smith and Lucy Smith, *English Gilds: the Original Ordinances of More Than One Hundred Early English Gilds* (London: Trübner, for the Early English Text Society, 1870; Oxford: Oxford University Press, for the Early English Text Society, 1963), 336.

[90] Smith, 285.

But beyond these efforts to provide quality goods to the consuming public, a medieval craftsman participated in social life by means of his guild membership. "The gild chantry, the provision of prayers and masses for deceased brethren, and the performance of pageants and mystery plays on the great feasts were no less functions of the gild than the common banquet, the regulation of work and wages, the giving of assistance to fellow gild-men in sickness or misfortune and the right to participate in the government of the city."[91]

In fact, a guild member saw himself as connected to the larger society by means of his participation in his guild. As Christopher Dawson further declared,

> Thus the medieval city was a community of communities in which the same principles of corporate rights and chartered liberties applied equally to the whole and to the parts. For the medieval idea of liberty, which finds it highest expression in the life of the free cities, was not the right of the individual to follow his own will, but the privilege of sharing in a highly organized form of corporate life which possessed its own constitution and rights of self-government. In many cases this constitution was hierarchical and authoritarian, but as every corporation had its own rights in the life of the city, so every individual had his place and his rights in the life of the gild.[92]

---

[91] Christopher Dawson, *Religion and the Rise of Western Culture* (New York: Sheed & Ward, 1950), 207.
[92] Dawson, 206.

This is in contrast to the modern notion that each person stands over against the state as an individual, and that far from being "a community of communities," the state is a community of individuals or, better, a mere collection of individuals, and that the state exists only to safeguard the material interests of those individuals. Such a conception of life, both social and individual, has numerous implications both in the economic sphere and otherwise, some of which we have already discussed. The Church's social doctrine has addressed this understanding of social existence directly, especially as it relates to economic matters. But however much the institutions of the modern world, in contrast to those of the Middle Ages, facilitate the vice of greed, it is also necessary to focus on how the attitudes and desires of each one of us also affect how we live.

This was obvious to the medieval Catholic mind, as it should be obvious to the Catholic mind of today. In fact, in modern Catholic social teaching, the same precept is inculcated, the precept that we should remember that life is ultimately not about possessing things. Pope Saint Paul VI, in the encyclical *Populorum Progressio*, pointed out that "increased possession is not the ultimate goal of nations nor of individuals. All growth is ambivalent. It is essential if man is to develop as a man, but in a way it imprisons man if he considers it the supreme good, and it restricts his vision. . . . The exclusive pursuit of possessions thus becomes an obstacle to individual fulfilment and to man's true greatness. Both for nations and for individual men, avarice is the most evident form of moral underdevelopment."[93]

---

[93]　Pope Paul VI, *Populorum Progressio* (March 26, 1967), no. 19.

Pope Saint John Paul II offered a remarkably penetrating analysis of the various kinds of goods and our desires for them in his encyclical *Centesimus Annus*.

> To call for an existence which is qualitatively more satisfying is of itself legitimate, but one cannot fail to draw attention to the new responsibilities and dangers connected with this phase of history. The manner in which new needs arise and are defined is always marked by a more or less appropriate concept of the human person and of the person's true good. A given culture reveals its overall understanding of life through the choices it makes in production and consumption. It is here that *the phenomenon of consumerism* arises. In singling out new needs and new means to meet them, one must be guided by a comprehensive picture of the person which respects all the dimensions of his being and which subordinates his material and instinctive dimensions to his interior and spiritual ones. If, on the contrary, a direct appeal is made to human instincts—while ignoring in various ways the reality of the person as intelligent and free—then *consumer attitudes and lifestyles* can be created which are objectively improper and often damaging to the person's physical and spiritual health. . . .
>
> It is not wrong to want to live better; what is wrong is a style of life which is presumed to be better when it is directed towards "having" rather than "being," and which wants to have more, not in order to be more but in order to spend life in enjoyment as an end in itself.[94]

---

[94] Pope John Paul II, *Centesimus Annus*, no. 36.

In defining ourselves by our possession and use of the latest gadgets, we are bearing witness to a particular "concept of the human person and of the person's true good," but a concept that deforms the human person and stunts our purpose in living. A healthy use of material possessions would be characterized not only by a necessary detachment but also, perhaps more importantly, by a skepticism and hesitation about embracing every new thing merely because it is new or faddish or appears to offer advantages over what we had previously.

"In singling out new needs and new means to meet them, one must be guided by a comprehensive picture of the person which respects all the dimensions of his being." Cell phones, for example, are not simply more convenient means for contacting people, but also have implications for the ways we interact with others, for our work culture, for family life, for our friendships, for our desires for instant gratification— despite their utility in facilitating communication, what do they say about the "comprehensive picture of the person" which our culture possesses? We ought to avoid dividing the human person or human life into distinct and mostly unrelated aspects or activities and feel satisfied if we think we have rendered any of those aspects or activities faster or simpler. It is the "comprehensive picture of the person which respects all the dimensions of his being" upon which we must learn to focus if we are to prevent twenty-first-century man from being made a slave to devices and pursuits which are not based on a total picture of the good of the human personality.

Papal social teaching since Leo XIII has been nothing less than an attempt to apply this body of ethical principles to the radically new situation in which mankind finds itself. In a way, the specifics of the Church's social teachings are less important than the central fact that economic life must be redirected toward goals other than individual enrichment or even prosperity for the sake of prosperity. G. K. Chesterton expressed this in some colorful words: "The aim of human polity is human happiness. . . . There is no obligation on us to be richer, or busier, or more efficient, or more productive, or more progressive, or in any way worldlier or wealthier, if it does not make us happier."[95]

Chesterton, moreover, would be the first to admit that "human happiness" on this earth means nothing unless it is ultimately oriented toward eternal happiness in heaven. No activity in this world can rightly take place as if death were simply the end of our existence. This does not mean, as I said before, that every one of our actions has to have a directly spiritual end, but it does mean that it is wrong to ignore the question of our eternal destiny in anything that we do. We do not always have to be thinking about heaven or hell, but we had better not undertake anything here below with no reference whatsoever to those ultimate and final realities.

Although the fundamental direction of the economy is in a sense more important than the specific measures mandated or suggested in papal social teaching, nevertheless these latter are by no means unimportant. If we examine the contents of Catholic social teaching since Leo XIII's *Rerum Novarum* of 1891, we will see its coherence with the principles embodied in the medieval economic order.

---

[95] G. K. Chesterton, *The Outline of Sanity*, in *The Collected Works of G. K. Chesterton*, vol. 5 (San Francisco: Ignatius, 1987), 145.

The modern world sees the economy as grounded in strife, in each economic actor attempting to gain as much as possible for himself. The capitalist version of this places the competition between capital and labor or between individual producers. The Marxist version locates it in hostility between social classes. Catholic social teaching, however, holds a different view. There is a natural harmony in the economy, provided that those involved are willing to submit to a standard of justice rather than simply striving to acquire as much as possible. When the Church turned her attention explicitly to the modern social problem, Pope Leo XIII forcefully stressed this point:

> The great mistake that is made in the matter now under consideration, is to possess oneself of the idea that class is naturally hostile to class; that rich and poor are intended by nature to live at war with one another. So irrational and so false is this view, that the exact contrary is the truth. Just as the symmetry of the human body is the result of the disposition of the members of the body, so in a State it is ordained by nature that these two classes should exist in harmony and agreement, and should, as it were, fit into one another, so as to maintain the equilibrium of the body politic. Each requires the other; capital cannot do without labor nor labor without capital. Mutual agreement results in pleasantness and good order; perpetual conflict necessarily produces confusion and outrage.[96]

---

[96] Pope Leo XIII, *Rerum Novarum* (May 15, 1891), no. 19.

But in the fallen state of mankind, even if this principle of natural harmony is accepted, different groups will tend to have different estimations of the worth of their own contribution and the corresponding economic reward which they are entitled to. And, yes, this is certainly true. Given mankind's fallen nature, we can always expect some lack of agreement, some sources of strife to exist. But there is a sizeable difference between acknowledging this and, on the other hand, proclaiming that the economy is naturally a battlefield of conflicting interests. No doubt it can be difficult to reestablish concord between spouses who have a long history of quarreling, but if each of them is committed to the idea that fundamentally their interests are in harmony, it will certainly be easier than if each of them considers the other a threat or an enemy. So with the economy; so with all the departments of human life.

The harmony which we ought to desire in the economy must be founded on justice, for justice is the virtue which assigns to each person what is his due. If everyone receives his just due, then no one has any reasonable claim to protest. Justice does not require that everyone receive exactly the same, for there are many factors which ought to determine such outcomes, but it does posit a minimum which every worker deserves simply based on his humanity. Leo XIII noted:

> [A] man's labor is *necessary*; for without the results of labor a man cannot live; and self-conservation is a law of nature, which it is wrong to disobey. Now, if we were to consider labor merely so far as it is *personal*,

doubtless it would be within the workman's right to accept any rate of wages whatever; for in the same way as he is free to work or not, so he is free to accept a small remuneration or even none at all. But this is a mere abstract supposition; the labor of the working man is not only his personal attribute, but it is *necessary*; and this makes all the difference. The preservation of life is the bounden duty of each and all, and to fail therein is a crime. It follows that each one has a right to procure what is required in order to live; and the poor can procure it in no other way than by work and wages.[97]

And therefore, according to Pope Leo, "there is a dictate of nature more imperious and more ancient than any bargain between man and man, that the remuneration must be enough to support the wage-earner in reasonable and frugal comfort. If through necessity or fear of a worse evil, the workman accepts harder conditions because an employer or contractor will give him no better, he is the victim of force and injustice."[98]

Leo XIII and his successors, without denying the state's necessary role in establishing economic justice, looked in preference to other institutions to achieve that end. In the beginning of *Rerum Novarum*, Pope Leo laments the disappearance of the medieval guilds and subsequently calls for the establishment of groups representing both owners and workers to exercise many of the functions that the

---

[97] Pope Leo XIII, no. 44.
[98] Pope Leo XIII, no. 45.

guilds once did: "In order to supersede undue interference on the part of the State, especially as circumstances, times and localities differ so widely, it is advisable that recourse be had to societies or boards such as We shall mention presently, or to some other method of safeguarding the interests of wage-earners; the State to be asked for approval and protection."[99] His successors, especially Pius XI and Pius XII, supported Leo XIII's position with a more detailed analysis of the function of these institutions, and they were eventually widely called by the name of occupational groups or, in the United States, industry councils.

But the practices and institutions of the economy must always be subordinated to the demands of justice. With regard to private property, for example, Pope Pius XI noted that "when civil authority adjusts ownership to meet the needs of the public good it acts not as an enemy, but as the friend of private owners; for thus it effectively prevents the possession of private property, intended by Nature's Author in His Wisdom for the sustaining of human life, from creating intolerable burdens and so rushing to its own destruction. It does not therefore abolish, but protects private ownership, and far from weaking the right to private property, it gives it new strength."[100]

And even the notion of competitive markets, so beloved by adherents of the modern economy, cannot be the supreme principle of our economic activity.

---

[99] Pope Leo XIII, no. 45.
[100] Pope Pius XI, *Quadragesimo Anno*, no. 49.

Just as the unity of human society cannot be built
upon "class" conflict, so the proper ordering of economic affairs cannot be left to the free play of rug-
ged competition. From this source, as from a polluted
spring, have proceeded all the errors of the "individualistic" school. This school, forgetful or ignorant of
the social and moral aspects of economic activities,
regarded these as completely free and immune from
any intervention by public authority, for they would
have in the market place and in unregulated competition a principle of self-direction more suitable for
guiding them than any created intellect which might
intervene. Free competition, however, though justified
and quite useful within certain limits, cannot be an
adequate controlling principle in economic affairs.
This has been abundantly proved by the consequences
that have followed from the free rein given to these
dangerous individualistic ideas.[101]

Our economic appetite, like our sexual appetite, tends to
disorder and must be restrained, not simply by the private
virtue of each individual, or even by custom and public opinion, but by institutions, laws, and regulations. For as Pius
XI noted with regard to the emerging modern economic
order with its numerous injustices, "A stern insistence on
the moral law, enforced with vigor by civil authority, could
have dispelled or perhaps averted these enormous evils"[102]
that the modern world created or augmented.

---

[101] Pope Pius XI, no. 88.
[102] Pope Pius XI, no. 133.

While this sketch of the social teachings of the modern popes is by no means complete, it should be sufficient to show the continuity between their teaching and the medieval tradition. Economic activity is important both because we are so dependent on its products or results and because its spirit tends to color the whole of society and even determine its direction. An economy which has lost its purpose, which is not oriented toward the fulfillment of human needs, has the ability to corrupt other important activities or aspects of human life, including technology, the arts, and even leisure. In the next few chapters, we will look at some of these activities and how they have been perverted by modernity with its loss of an understanding of the inherent purpose of things and its widespread acceptance of greed as an acceptable motive for our actions.

CHAPTER FIVE

Knowledge or Science?

*"Any sufficiently advanced technology is
indistinguishable from magic."*[103]

—Arthur C. Clarke

The title of this chapter is a paradox and is meant to be. The word *science* is derived from the Latin *scientia*, primarily meaning "knowledge." How, then, could there be a contrast, much less a conflict, between the two? But as so much else in the modern world has been corrupted, so also the scientific endeavor, and in this case, it happened long before significant scientific activity reached the shores of this country. Perhaps the best way to introduce this subject is by citing the Anglican writer and scholar C. S. Lewis.

In his 1943 Riddell Memorial Lectures, published as *The Abolition of Man*, Lewis compared two seemingly very different human undertakings: science and magic.

> The serious magical endeavour and the serious scientific endeavour are twins: one was sickly and died, the other strong and throve. But they were twins. They

---

[103] Arthur C. Clarke, *Profiles of the Future* (New York: Warner, 1984), 26.

were born of the same impulse. . . . There is something which unites magic and applied science while separating both from the 'wisdom' of earlier ages. For the wise men of old the cardinal problem had been how to conform the soul to reality, and the solution had been knowledge, self-discipline, and virtue. For magic and applied science alike the problem is how to subdue reality to the wishes of men. . . . Bacon condemns those who value knowledge as an end it [sic] itself: this, for him, is to use as a mistress for pleasure what ought to be a spouse for fruit. The true object is to extend Man's power to the performance of all things possible.[104]

And he states further, "It might be going too far to say that the modern scientific movement was tainted from its birth: but I think that it was born in an unhealthy neighbourhood and at an inauspicious hour."[105]

This idea will probably come as a surprise to many readers. How could science, the careful observation and measurement of reality, be compared with magic, which is, at best, a primitive and haphazard attempt to manipulate poorly understood natural forces and, at worst, a compact with devils? The answer to this is that science, as conceived and practiced since the sixteenth century, and magic are both oriented toward power, toward results, toward manipulating the natural world according to man's will and desires.

---

[104] C. S. Lewis, *The Abolition of Man* (New York: Macmillan, 1947), 87–89.
[105] Lewis, 87–89.

Technology, not knowledge, is the real aim of this endeavor. And in fact, the founders of modern science were candid about their aims. Lewis mentioned Francis Bacon, whose ambition was nothing less than to refound all of human knowledge and to explicitly inaugurate a new science: "It is not possible to run a course aright when the goal itself has not been rightly placed. Now the true and lawful goal of the sciences is none other than this: that human life be endowed with new discoveries and powers."[106]

His younger contemporary, René Descartes, whose historical influence was much greater than that of Bacon, desired that "instead of that speculative philosophy which is taught in the Schools, we may find a practical philosophy by means of which . . . we can . . . render ourselves the masters and possessors of nature."[107]

This characteristic of modern science has, of course, been noted over and over again, and as one philosopher of science asserted, "Modern science is not so much the understanding of nature as the art of mastering nature."[108] Another contemporary philosopher speaks of such figures as Bacon and his collaborators in the following words: "The humility with regard to the cosmos that all previous civilizations took for granted in spite of their advanced sciences like mathematics and astronomy is incomprehensible for our moderns, whose vocabulary is

---

[106] Francis Bacon, *Novum Organum*, in *Selected Writings of Francis Bacon* (New York: Modern Library, 1955), 499.

[107] René Descartes, *Discourse on Method*, in *The Philosophical Works of Descartes*, vol. 1, (Cambridge: Cambridge University Press, 1975), 119.

[108] Jacob Klein, "Modern Rationalism," in *Lectures and Essays* (Annapolis: St. John's College, 1985), 60.

crowded with words like scientific conquest, the secrets of the universe solved because measured, the liquidation of myths and mysteries. The comments accompanying space exploration give the impression that we are detachable from the cosmos, and that we are entitled to colonize it, populate parts of its, exploit its mineral resources, and use it as a military, industrial base."[109]

Before considering what were the factors which led to this new kind of science, how the meaning of science was changed from *knowledge* to power over the natural world, one thing must be made clear: Technology as such—that is, devices and techniques to assist us in our legitimate activities—is not evil. If we had absolutely no technology, we would all need to dwell in caves, drink water with our cupped hands, and eat raw fruits and vegetables. As long as mankind has existed, we have had technology and technological improvements, nor is there anything wrong with improving the physical quality of our lives. What is wrong, in the first place, is supposing that the highest use of our God-given intellect lies in inventing microwave ovens or iPads. Compared with contemplation of God and the truths of the Faith, or even the truths of the natural order, these inventions are of little importance. And secondly, just because a certain device makes some process faster, cheaper, or simpler, it does not follow that this will necessarily improve the overall quality of human life. Technology is not neutral. It is true that most inventions can be used either for good or evil, but it is also true that given the weakness of fallen mankind,

---

[109] Thomas Molnar, *The Emerging Atlantic Culture* (New Brunswick: Transaction, 1994), 72.

we will tend to embrace whatever makes a process faster or cheaper, regardless of its impact on social life or the natural environment. And lastly, the spirit of modern technology is on the whole very different from the spirit of earlier technology. Instead of working with the natural powers with which God has endowed His creation, we think nothing of twisting and extorting whatever potentialities we can discover in the created things around us. We look upon ourselves as conquerors of, rather than collaborators with, the natural world. So while we should recognize that technology as such is not evil, like any other creation or product of fallen man, it does not always necessarily serve our genuine well-being.

If it is the case that science, as the modern world understands it, is a project whose primary interest is in power, how did this come about? How did such a momentous change take place in our civilization? The short answer is that it was accomplished by the overthrow of the philosophy of Aristotle and of medieval Thomism—"that speculative philosophy which is taught in the Schools," as Descartes put it—in favor of a philosophy grounded ultimately in the thought of William of Ockham and other nominalists. The end result of Ockham's philosophy "is to replace a hierarchy of *being* with a hierarchy based on *will* or power."[110] The American Aristotelian philosopher Henry Veatch summed up this intellectual revolution in saying that "the very rise of so-called modern science and modern philosophy was originally associated—certainly in the minds of men like Galileo and Descartes—with a determined repudiation of Aristotle:

---

[110] Terence L. Nichols, *The Sacred Cosmos: Christian Faith and the Challenge of Naturalism* (Grand Rapids, MI: Brazos Press, 2003), 39.

it was precisely his influence which it was thought necessary to destroy, root and branch, before what we now know as science and philosophy in the modern mode could get off the ground."[111]

In the brilliant first chapter of his *English Literature in the Sixteenth Century*, C. S. Lewis sketched the crucial role of mathematics in this process and its effects on man's relationship with nature:

> What was fruitful in the thought of the new scientists was the bold use of mathematics in the construction of hypotheses, tested not by observation simply but by controlled observation of phenomena that could be precisely measured. On the practical side it was this that delivered Nature into our hands. And on our thoughts and emotions . . . it was destined to have profound effects. By reducing Nature to her mathematical elements it substituted a mechanical for a genial or animistic conception of the universe. The world was emptied, first of her indwelling spirits, then of her occult sympathies and antipathies, finally of her colours, smells, and tastes. . . . The result was dualism rather than materialism. The mind, on whose ideal constructions the whole method depended, stood over against its object in ever sharper dissimilarity. Man, with his new powers became rich like Midas but all that he touched had gone dead and cold.[112]

---

[111] Henry Veatch, *Aristotle, a Contemporary Appreciation* (Bloomington: Indiana University, 1974), 4.

[112] C. S. Lewis, *English Literature in the Sixteenth Century* (Oxford: Clarendon Press, 1954), 3–4.

But modern science *must* work by "reducing Nature to her mathematical elements." For whatever cannot be understood mathematically or quantitatively cannot so easily be manipulated. But when we know something only insofar as it is subject to mathematics—subject to measurement, that is—we know it only in part. In fact, we know it only in so far as we can make use of it. Whatever cannot be understood in this way is, in practice, disregarded by modern science because its methodology is unable to deal with it.

The Catholic philosopher Etienne Gilson explains this further:

> According to St. Thomas Aquinas, the physical order was essentially made up of "natures," that is to say, of active principles, which were the cause of the motions and various operations of their respective matters. In other words, each nature, or form, was essentially an energy, an act. Now it is an obvious fact that such a world was no fit subject for a purely mechanical interpretation of physical change; dimensions, positions and distances are by themselves clear things; they can be measured and numbered; but those secret energies that had been ascribed to bodies by Aristotle and St. Thomas, could not be submitted to any kind of calculation. Should they be allowed to stay there, . . . there would remain in nature something confused and obscure, and in science itself, a standing element of unintelligibility. As a geometer, who wanted physics to become a department of his universal mathematics, Descartes could not possibly tolerate such a nuisance.

Forms, natures and energies had to be eliminated then from the physical world, so that there should be nothing left but extension and an always equal amount of motion caused by God.[113]

This methodological defect applies also to those sciences that deal directly with man. What are usually called in this country the social sciences, and in many European intellectual traditions the human sciences, such as psychology or economics, insofar as they seek to mimic the quantitative methods of physics or chemistry, likewise try to disregard whatever cannot be measured. Hence psychological experiments that treat subjects as simply reflex machines, or the ubiquitous graphs used by most economists to chart our propensity to buy or sell at a certain price. And it is true that certain aspects of man in the mass can be captured by such methods, just as we can understand certain aspects of the natural world with these same kinds of methods. But the endpoint of such a manipulative approach, as applied to humans, would seem to have been reached with B. F. Skinner's behaviorism in the twentieth century, a method that reduced the human person to simply a reflex of stimuli and responses to be manipulated according to the desires of whoever has the power to do so.

If we accept that this turning of science away from its original classical and medieval goal of knowledge was a colossal error, what can we say about the omnipresent technology which has resulted from this? I do not suppose that there is

---

[113] Etienne Gilson, *The Unity of Philosophical Experience* (Westminster, MD: Christian Classics, 1982), 203–4.

anyone who would argue that human social life ought to be subservient to technology—that is, that technology should set the standards and pace of human life—rather than the other way around. For it is simply a commonplace that technology exists to serve us. We are supposed to be its masters, technology to be our servant. But is this really always, or even usually, the case?

Above, I stated that technology is not neutral. Given the fallen state of man, that our unbridled passions and lower desires so easily get out of control, we are not only apt to misuse technology directly, as in using a gun to commit a crime, but historically we have allowed technology to shape our societies with hardly any real discussion about whether this was for the good or not.

Take as an example the automobile. People have sought to move about since we have existed, and so it seemed clear that any device that facilitated such movement was for the good. But did we foresee, or even try to foresee, what some of its results would be? Did we desire the physical separation of fathers from their families during the work day? Or the exorbitant growth of cities, with so much space taken up by parking lots and superhighways? Or the ease with which people could leave their homes and neighborhoods, thus weakening community ties? Perhaps, after serious consideration, we might have concluded that all these ills were worth it if we could move about faster and simpler, that speed and ease of movement were nearly supreme goods to which other and lesser goods should be subordinated. But in fact we never even considered the question. We never had a national conversation about whether this new technology would be, on the whole, a blessing or a curse, or something in-between.

Cars were produced in order to make money; people who could afford them bought them to get about more easily; soon, automobile owners pressured local, state, and ultimately federal legislators to build or improve roads and furnish other amenities to make their traveling quicker and safer and more fun. An entire industry, or rather, a set of industries, arose in response, and soon automobile traffic became so much a part of our way of life that it seems impossible to reverse it, even if we wanted to. Can we honestly say that in the case of motor cars we are the masters and they are the servants when, in most places, it is impossible to live without a car, however much someone might disdain their use?

Besides cars, the same is true of all or almost all modern technology. Marketers promote it with such appeal and alacrity. As a result, its desirability is simply assumed by our entire culture and inculcated in us from our earliest education; humanity does not stand much of a chance. To be sure, I am not here taking a position pro or con on any particular invention. I am simply calling our attention to the fact that it is slightly absurd to say that modern technology is our servant when, in fact, it is largely the other way around. We do not carefully consider whether a new invention is for our good or not. They conquer us and impose their use on us due not only to their creators and promoters but also to the disorderly intellects and wills and appetites of the fallen human race.

It goes without saying that new technology also feeds the Prosperity Gospel. The latest technology creates desires we never had before. Middle school kids must now have the latest iPhones; teenagers seek the latest SUV. And as a result, parents are forced to work even harder to maintain a prosperous lifestyle. But Our Lord was clear: "Do not labor for the food which perishes, but for the food which endures to eternal life, which the Son of man will give to you; for on him has God the Father set his seal" (Jn 6:27).

How is this indictment of technological developments connected with our theme of the general lack of a publicly acknowledged purpose which afflicts modern life? God has largely indicated how man is to live by the way He created us. By endowing us with certain powers and propensities, He shows us what our life, individual and social, is to be like. And as I said above, unless we are to live in caves and eat raw fruits and vegetables, we need technology of some kind. Moreover, there is no reason why this technology cannot continue to develop as long as the world lasts, provided, however, that it develops as our servant and not our master. But if we allow it to become our master, then surely we are acquiescing to an inversion of values that is not in accordance with how God created us. For Christians ought to recognize that even amidst the goods of this world, we cannot lose sight of our eternal home, lest we forfeit that forever. Thus, if technology is allowed to run riot and determine how we live—is permitted to shape our families, our cities, our nations—that certainly is not why God created us with the capacity to make and use technology. He did not intend it to rule us, and to suppose that He did is simply an absurdity.

Technology has developed and improved throughout man's history. But with the technological slant of science, recent centuries have greatly accelerated this development, and moreover, the newer sorts of technology have had more of a transforming impact on human life as a whole, as we saw with the automobile. So again, it is the unchaining of technology from its purpose as simply a subordinate part of human social life that is the problem here. Only when technology, like every other aspect of our earthly life, is seen as part of a whole, as part of a hierarchy at whose apex is eternal life with God, can these various aspects function properly and promote the true welfare of man. If not, they become distractions from our own end and have the potential even to thwart our very attainment of that end.

CHAPTER SIX

The Corrupting
of Education:
If You're So Smart, How
Come You Ain't Rich?

In April 1937, Robert M. Hutchins, the thirty-eight-year-old president of the University of Chicago, gave an address to the National Catholic Educational Association Midwest Regional Meeting in which he charged that Catholic education in the United States had "imitated the worst features of secular education"—namely, "athleticism and collegiatism," the latter being "the production of well-tubbed young Americans." Hutchins was not a Catholic, but he used our own principles against us. "What I say," he continued, "is that Catholic education is not Catholic enough. The Catholic Church has the longest intellectual tradition of any institution in the contemporary world, the only uninterrupted tradition and the only explicit tradition. . . . What I say is that this tradition must not be merely an ideal, but must be practiced."[114]

---

[114] In Frank L. Christ and Gerard E. Sherry, eds., *American Catholicism and*

Here we have a comprehensive indictment of Catholic education, especially higher education, in the United States. This indictment is twofold: a significant departure from the almost two millennia long history of Catholic thought and a consequent embrace of contemporary educational goals, standards, and methods as those were formulated and practiced by the surrounding disintegrating Protestant culture. Hutchins, who became president of Chicago before his thirtieth birthday, is probably remembered most for his advocacy of the Great Books movement and his elimination of the football program at Chicago. The Great Books movement, which bases itself on study and discussion of the heritage of Western thought, as that is embodied in some of its greatest intellectual monuments, necessarily finds itself in dialogue with the Catholic intellectual tradition, for Western thought for centuries coincided almost completely with Catholic thought. Any curriculum that seeks an understanding of the evolution of the European mind, as well as its later developments in the Western Hemisphere, can hardly avoid a close engagement with Catholic thought.

But when we look at American higher education, we see other influences at work, influences which have largely prevailed over the course of time. These chiefly have born fruit in the elective system, which, depending on the institution, allows significant student choice in shaping a course of study, and the incorporation of all kinds of technical or "practical" subjects into the curriculum, from business and

the Intellectual Ideal (New York: Appleton-Century-Crofts, 1961), 109–11. Originally published in *College Newsletter, Midwest Regional Unit, NCEA,* May 1937.

marketing to some that border on absurdity. Here is part of the description of the Turfgrass Science program at Ohio State University: "Are you someone who enjoys being outdoors? Do you have a passion for sports and science? Then you may consider a career in Turfgrass Science. This exciting career path will teach you all about Turfgrass science and management of all different sports settings."[115]

This proliferation of fields of study, all apparently of equal value and status and organized according to no intellectual hierarchy except that of the alphabet, has no unifying intellectual principle. Indeed, in a rare moment of candor, Robert Burns, then president of the College (now University) of the Pacific, actually wrote, "The curriculum has become diversified; there are numerous electives. Few study the same courses or sit under the same professors. . . . So, in this period of intellectual and social disintegration of the American college, all unite in football. . . . Football has become more than a spectacle; it has become a symbol; it has become one of the great intangibles not only of college but of our American life. Actually, if you want to look at it on a higher level, football has become the spiritual core of the modern campus."[116]

If a university sees its need for a "spiritual core," and lacks the will or the courage to say that some subjects are more fundamental than others, that its "spiritual core" should be

---

[115] "The Value of a Certificate," Buckeye Turf (website), July 19, 2018, buckeyeturf.osu.edu/node/94.
[116] Quoted in Robert Hutchins, "College Football is an Infernal Nuisance," *Sports Illustrated*, October 18, 1954, https://vault.si.com/vault/1954/10/18 /college-football-is-an-infernal-nuisance.

found in its study of theology and philosophy, perhaps it is appropriate that it chooses football, after all. For at least it is acknowledging the reality that American higher education has little interest in cultivating a lasting life of the mind in its students.

While the attempt to confer academic status on a potpourri of glorified trades and other occupations—however legitimate many of them may be in themselves as ways of earning a living—what of the liberal arts themselves? How have they fared with the triumph of the multiversity and its smaller collegiate imitations?

To answer this question, let us look further at Robert Hutchins's critique. In discussing what he called the "worst features of secular education" that Catholics had copied, Hutchins noted *athleticism* as among the top two. And he continued, "The reason for athleticism is obvious—secular universities are supported by their alumni who understand football and not much else."[117] If the graduates of secular institutions—and this undoubtedly included numerous persons who had studied the liberal arts—"understand football and not much else," what does this say about the enduring effect of the education given by these colleges and universities? In 1937, the American curriculum was in general probably more traditional than it is today; that is, the requirements for majors were stricter and the courses offered probably less wide-ranging. But the result was not the creation of a literate group of citizens who at least strove to keep up an intellectual life in their spare moments. Hutchins again: "If the object of a university is to produce good athletes

---

[117] Hutchins, 110.

or well-tubbed Americans or to secure its graduates good jobs, what is the point of intellectual training? Abstract problems have no relation at all to those aims. Consequently, intellectual training has been driven out of the curriculum."[118]

Sadly, it must be admitted that probably the overwhelming majority of liberal arts graduates seldom read serious books after they complete their formal education. They have obtained their degrees and some kind of qualification that allows them to get a job and, they hope, to have a successful and lucrative career. That is all they ever really wanted. While they were students, some of them doubtless made a simulation of being scholars or intellectuals, but when they emerged from the scholastic atmosphere of formal education, that simulation rapidly vanished and they sunk back into the routines and patterns of American life. The result? "In no other country in the world can first-rate doctors and lawyers be encountered who know nothing outside of their own profession. Culture, not having a cash value, is disesteemed."[119]

An attitude toward education that sees it as simply a ticket to a good job will eventually lead to viewing college via a cost/benefit calculus, as expressed, for example, in the concept of *return on investment.*

> With the cost of college rising each year and questionable career prospects awaiting college graduates, some people are wondering if a college education is still worth it. If you took all the money you would spend

---

[118] Hutchins, 110.

[119] Theodore Maynard, *The Story of American Catholicism* (New York: Macmillan, 1941), 586.

on a college degree and invested it, would you come out ahead? Are college loans worth it?

One of the ways to figure out if a degree is worth the money is to calculate the return on investment (ROI) of a college education. The ROI is a metric that measures the effectiveness of the return on an investment but also compares it to other investments during a similar time period.

ROI is calculated by dividing the benefit of return by the cost of the investment. The result is expressed as a percent or a ratio. In this article we look at the return on investment for college degrees based on a few different factors and compare them to other investments.[120]

Nor do those who are involved in promoting higher education look upon it in a fundamentally different manner. As the Indiana Commission for Higher Education expressed it, "An investment in higher education may be the smartest purchase Hoosiers ever make. The value of a college degree is undeniable . . . more opportunities, higher earnings, and greater job security."[121]

No one would deny the high and rising cost of American higher education nor the increasing burden of student loans. More on this later. But neither of these factors, important as they are, is the point. The point, rather, is that in the United

---

[120] Eric Rosenberg, "College Tuition vs. Investing: Is It Worth It?," Investopedia, June 15, 2022, https://www.investopedia.com/articles/personal-finance/062515/college-tuition-vs-investing-it-worth-it.asp.

[121] "Return on Investment Dashboard," Indiana Commission for Higher Education, accessed August 25, 2022, in.gov/che/college-value-reports/return-on-investment-dashboard/.

States, the value of higher education is seen exclusively, or nearly so, in terms of one thing: money. Will a degree help you get a better job, earn more money? Will it pay for itself? In asking whether a degree in engineering is better than a degree in art history, one thing only is meant: which one will generate more income. Education is simply an investment like any other investment and must be judged accordingly. And our common attitude toward investments, as expressed by the Nobel prize winning economist Paul Samuelson, is also quite clear: "There is one rule that gives correct answers to all investment decisions: Calculate the present value resulting from each possible decision. Then always act so as to maximize present value. In this way you will have more wealth to spend whenever and however you like."[122]

It is surely odd that such an extensive and expensive enterprise as higher education, with its panoply of lecture halls, libraries, and laboratories, with its faculty members with multiple and impressive degrees, and which offers such an array of courses that might help initiate students into the Western intellectual heritage, and which on occasion even likes to hark back to its venerable roots in the medieval university, should, in the end, be reduced to an investment decision, or to a chance to obtain "more opportunities, higher earnings, and greater job security." Seldom is there a word about becoming acquainted with our civilizational heritage, about learning to think more clearly, even about becoming a better and more thoughtful citizen. When confused and stupid protestors

---

[122] Paul Samuelson, *Microeconomics*, 17th ed. (Boston: McGraw-Hill Irwin, 2001), 274.

chanted some years ago, "Hey, hey, ho, ho, Western culture's got to go," they needn't have troubled themselves, for serious study of Western culture had pretty much departed long ago.

Of course, I do not deny the real burden of college costs and student debt and the consequent anxiety about careers. This is a problem that certainly needs to be addressed. What I object to is that this burden is used as an excuse for tossing aside all intellectual concerns, which are assumed to be, at best, a nice avocation for those with leisure and taste for such pursuits, but not of any importance in the real world. Liberal arts colleges are reduced to trying to prove that the study of philosophy or literature or history actually equips one for the corporate world better than, say, the study of business. Boethius, Chaucer, Shakespeare—wonderful ways to exercise and train the mind so that afterwards humanities graduates can spend their time concocting marketing campaigns for dish soap or dog food.

It is not unreasonable to hope that one's studies might be of some help in the direction of making a living. But must all the effort of study and learning, learning—for those who study the liberal arts—ostensibly occupied with the truth about ultimate questions and with our intellectual and cultural tradition, simply be forgotten upon graduation? The French Dominican Antonin Sertillanges, in his remarkable book, *The Intellectual Life*, offers as counsel to everyone that "after a first early and toilsome training no one acts wisely if he lets his mind fall gradually back into its primitive ignorance."[123] If liberal education as that imparted in this

---

[123] Antonin Sertillanges, *The Intellectual Life* (Westminster, MD: Christian Classics, 1980), 3–4.

country has the effect that it was traditionally advertised to have, would not a greater percentage of graduates at least make some effort, in their spare moments anyway, to prevent their minds falling back into "primitive ignorance"? Would they not at least aspire to understand something more than football in their later years? Would we not have avoided the stigma of being the only country in the world in which "first-rate doctors and lawyers [can] be encountered who know nothing outside of their own profession"?

What, however, is the context and background of this understanding of the aims of education as being merely for the sake of a lucrative career? And why this disdain for real learning on the part of those who presumably should be among its most loyal supporters? On the one hand, the American preoccupation with money and worldly success militates against a genuine life of the mind. And on the other hand, very much acquaintance with our cultural heritage, Christian or pagan, will expose students to values very different from money and the things that money can buy. A love of learning will reveal a world wider, deeper, and of more significance than the world in which the *summum bonum* is to "maximize present value" so that "you will have more wealth to spend whenever and however you like." Not only the entire Christian tradition but the greatest pagan thinkers of classical antiquity would have regarded such a sentiment as an utter perversion of the human soul. That it can be said with a straight face here speaks volumes about the state of *our* souls.

Connected with our national emphasis on moneymaking is the assumption that education is an individual matter, and that each person should pursue an education in order to achieve his own private ends, whatever they might be. Education is thus robbed of its inherent purpose, and made simply a means for whatever anyone might desire it to be. Pope Pius XI, in his 1929 encyclical on education, *Divini Illius Magistri*, taught exactly the opposite: "Education is essentially a social and not a mere individual activity."[124] Father Sertillanges, whom I have already quoted, spoke of the benefits accruing to Christ's Mystical Body from each person's fulfillment of his assigned task, especially those called to higher studies:

> Christianized humanity is made up of various personalities, no one of which can refuse to function without impoverishing the group and without depriving the eternal Christ of a part of His kingdom. Christ reigns by unfolding Himself in men. Every life of one of His members is a characteristic moment of His duration; every individual man and Christian is an instance, incommunicable, unique, and therefore necessary, of the extension of the "spiritual body." If you are designated as a light bearer, do not go and hide under the bushel the gleam or the flame expected from you in the house of the Father of all. Love truth and its fruits of life, for yourself and for others; devote to study and to the profitable use of study the best part of your time and your heart.[125]

Every society that has ever existed, from the most primitive to the most cultured, has had some kind of education of

---

[124] Pope Pius XI, *Divini Illius Magistri* (December 31, 1929), no. 11.
[125] Sertillanges, *The Intellectual Life*, 5.

its youth. Whether it was teaching young men to be better hunters or founding universities for the study of philosophy and theology as in the Middle Ages, it was always clear that the formation of the next generation was a crucial concern of society as a whole. But why? If we look upon higher education as nothing more than "the smartest purchase Hoosiers ever make," if it provides nothing more than "opportunities, higher earnings, and greater job security" for individuals, why should it be much of a concern to Church or state? Why did the medieval Church spend scarce resources not only building churches but also founding universities? Why does the state of Indiana itself devote large sums of money to maintaining its publicly-supported universities? Simply in order to indulge us with "more opportunities, higher earnings, and greater job security"? Whatever may be the reason why colleges and universities continue doggedly with their activities today, originally they were founded because it was believed that they offered something important to both Church and state. The medieval universities, which certainly did not have programs in Turfgrass Science or marketing, were considered so important to Christendom that even in the midst of its life and death struggle with Islam, time and money was spent on studying the seven liberal arts, philosophy, and theology. Our ancestors recognized that education had primarily a social end, that it was necessary for the flourishing of a truly Christian civilization. No doubt medieval graduates usually obtained personal benefits from their studies, but at the time, no one was crass enough to offer that as the only or chief justification for obtaining a university education.

In fact, the entire elective system is based on an understanding of higher education that sees its benefits as primarily *individual*. Since I am making an investment, a very important and costly investment, then surely I am entitled to study whatever I want to—for it's *my* money and *my* time. The roots of this, however, go much deeper than simply the aims of education. If religion and morality are purely private affairs, then the aims that each person sets for himself, whether that be money or pleasure or learning or holiness, are necessarily his own concerns. He seeks an education in order to further his private aims, none of which, as far as public culture is concerned, is any better than any other. And in a society in which the love of money runs rampant, for most people it turns out to be "more opportunities, higher earnings, and greater job security."

We can see from this the intimate connection between the ideals which a society holds and how they work themselves out in the most diverse fields of human endeavor. As long as education is conceived of as "a mere individual activity," it will follow that since its aims are purely private, a curriculum which allows considerable student choice will be the standard. Students are consumers, it is their money (or their parents') which they are spending, and it follows that they should have maximum say in how this money is spent.

There is one other thing I should mention for the sake of completeness. In recent decades at many institutions, humanities departments have been captured by ideologues of ever more and more noxious theories: queer studies, gender studies, varieties of critical theory, and so on. And this has driven some students away from the humanities who concluded, based on the knowledge they had, that subjects such as philosophy, literature, or history were nothing more than nonsense, nonsense dressed up in pretentious pseudo-intellectual garb. But of course this is not the case, and the remedy for such perversions of the liberal arts is not to abandon or neglect those subjects but to study and teach them correctly. Moreover, as we have seen, the neglect of the liberal arts long predates the hegemony of this latest version of academic nonsense. So while in some cases the appropriation of the liberal arts by ideologues has been partly responsible for declining enrollments, this by no means explains everything. For that, we need to look to the larger cultural situation, as we have been doing.

Education implies the imparting of knowledge of some kind. In today's world, it is the knowledge supplied by the natural sciences that enjoys the most prestige. We have already seen how the pursuit of the sciences in the modern world became an effort to gain not wisdom but power over nature for the sake of convenience in living. But obviously this did not stop with either science or education. Let us next look at how modernity has affected the arts and their place in the hierarchy of society.

CHAPTER SEVEN

Art

The word *art* has several related meanings. It can mean the inborn skill or talent an individual has, or his acquired technique and knowledge. Or it can mean the products of that skill or knowledge, the actual concrete things that an artist makes. When we think of such artistic products, we commonly divide them into two groups: the useful arts and the fine arts. We speak of the art of cooking, woodworking, and so on, and no one would deny that these are useful for human life, that they have inherent or intrinsic purposes. But then we also have the fine arts—painting, sculpture, music, and the like—arts which we are not accustomed to call useful and which we might hesitate to say have an inherent purpose of their own. Art for art's sake seems to capture the usual understanding of their role in human life. Or perhaps some would say that their purpose is to exhibit or manifest beauty. But is this really exactly the case? What is the correct way to understand the arts and their purpose?

Saint Thomas Aquinas has an interesting passage in which he remarks that an artist intends the best arrangement or disposition of his material according to the purpose of what he is making. And he continues, "And if such a disposition has with it some defect, the artist is not concerned; just as the artist who makes a saw for cutting makes it from iron, so that it is suitable for cutting; he does not care to make it from glass, which is a more beautiful material, because such beauty would be a hindrance to its purpose."[126]

Well, of course, one might say. Who would ever make a saw out of glass or some other decorative but weak material? Since a saw is meant for cutting, obviously glass is not an appropriate material. But the point goes deeper. It is the purpose of a thing that determines its appropriate material or the appropriate arrangement of that material. Glass may be more beautiful, but it is not suitable for a saw. This same principle holds true in all the arts, both useful and fine. In writing music for the sacred liturgy, for example, a composer must keep in mind the actual use to which his music will be put. He seeks beauty, no doubt, but he subordinates beauty to the necessities of the actual celebration of the liturgy. So, for example, he must not make his setting for the Mass over-long, even though that might prolong its beauty, or require such a large number of musicians as to make it unsuitable for use in a church.

Now, before about the middle of the eighteenth century, most products of the fine arts were made for some obvious social purpose. Music, painting, and sculpture adorned the liturgy, other music was written for dancing or military marches, and public monuments commemorated some historical event or sought to give honor and glory to a ruler. In all of these types, the artist naturally aimed at as much

---

[126] Thomas Aquinas, *Summa Theologiae*, I, q. 91, a. 3.

beauty as his talent and technique could provide, but always in subordination to its inherent purpose, whether the celebration of Mass or a good dance step. They did not aim at beauty divorced from the social end which regulated how they would work and for the sake of which they exercised their art. They sought beauty, yes, but not beauty in the abstract. How they would seek beauty was subordinate to the intended use of whatever they were making. Otherwise, "such beauty would be a hindrance to its purpose," to the purpose of their work.

Another important feature to be noted about the arts during this time was the shared intellectual framework that all classes of society accepted as valid—namely, the Christian faith, originally, of course, as taught by the Catholic Church but which continued to provide a common social belief system for some decades even in Protestant countries. "There was available for imitation a universally valid conceptual reality, whose order the artist could not tamper with. The subject matter of art was prescribed by those who commissioned works of art, which were not created, as in bourgeois society, on speculation. . . . As long as there was general agreement as to what were the worthiest subjects for art, the artist was relieved of the necessity to be original."[127]

But in the eighteenth century, this started to change. The previously universally accepted Christian understanding of reality began to unravel, and hence artists needed new inspiration. They started to pursue beauty simply as such, and they created sculptures, paintings, and music which no

---

[127] Clement Greenberg, *Art and Culture* (Boston: Beacon Press, 1961), 16.

longer had a public purpose, no longer fulfilled a role within society. As a result, special places and times had to be created in which these new types of art objects could be seen or heard: museums, galleries, concert halls, and so forth. These artistic works were no longer part of the larger round of human social life; they depended on these special venues and events in order to become known to the public.

Now, is this anything to be deplored? Are we not indebted to the composers and painters and sculptors of the late eighteenth and the nineteenth centuries for innumerable works of beauty, works that have no specific social role, certainly, but that are part of the glories of our civilization? To take music alone, there are symphonies and concertos, even works written in the form of sacred music that were never intended to be used in the actual liturgy due to their excessive length or the size of the orchestra required or the unsuitability of their style. But they include many works of the highest beauty. What could possibly be wrong with that?

In the first place, there is a rather obvious problem with such an approach to art. As I previously mentioned, before the eighteenth century, most products of the fine arts, because they were integrated into social life, were seen or heard by vast numbers of the population. Sculptures might decorate public squares or buildings frequented by the citizenry, town or guild halls, the outsides of palaces, and so on. Anyone hearing Mass might also hear the music of a Palestrina or a Lassus. Even in Protestant countries, this was often true, and much of the music of Bach was written for and used in actual worship services.

But this changed. Going to classical music concerts or art galleries is now mostly the province of select classes. Of course, such events are open to anyone who can afford them, but everyone does not go to them. They exacerbate the class division of society, and even more importantly, they have facilitated the rise of what is often called popular culture, but in reality is *mass* culture, made possible by developing technology, and almost always inferior not only to the classical arts but to the folk or genuine popular arts of our ancestors.

There is a more important and more fundamental reason, however, to regret the changed role that the arts have in society. This is their lack of purpose, the theme that we have been considering throughout this book. Recall that music written for the celebration of the liturgy or for dancing or marching had to subordinate itself to those purposes. A good beat might be fine for the latter but not appropriate for church music. So a composer, say, could not simply follow his genius or his whims wherever they might lead him—he had to remember his purpose, and also his patrons, for they had commissioned the work for a specific purpose and would not willingly pay for something which did not fulfill that purpose. Thus, the fine arts were kept in bounds by their being embedded in the overall social life of the community, just as was the case with our economic activity and all other aspects of human life.

As the fine arts became more and more detached from some broader social purpose, at first, this had no effect on artists' pursuit of beauty. The great works of nineteenth-century art include some of the greatest music and other artistic works of our heritage. But this did not last. Divorced from a social role, no longer bound by patrons who simply wanted suitable artistic adornment for the several activities of mankind, practitioners of all the arts turned inward. They became bored and sought novelty in styles and forms that most people would not call beautiful, eventually taking delight in deliberate ugliness. An artist was now seen as someone who expressed his individuality, who followed his whims, and soon as someone who stood over against society rather than as someone who was a part of society and performed an important role in it. The lonely and sometimes starving artist in his garret now became a stock figure.

The point here, as I have already said, was the loss of any public or inherent purpose for artists and the arts. Devoid of such purpose, art can become anything an artist wants. Consequently, nonsense and ugliness have as much right as anything else to the name of art, since all is now an expression of individuality governed only by the artist's subjective purpose or his desire to express what he regards as his individuality.

At first, artists turned their attention to the process of artistic creation itself: "Picasso, Braque . . . derive their chief inspiration from the medium they work in. The excitement of their art seems to lie most of all in its pure preoccupation with the invention and arrangement of spaces, surfaces, shapes, colors, etc. . . . Gide's most ambitious book is a novel about the writing of a novel, and that Joyce's *Ulysses* and *Finnegans Wake* seem to be . . . the reduction of experience to expression for the sake of expression, the expression mattering more than what is being expressed."[128]

---

[128] Greenberg, *Art and Culture*, 7–8.

As things developed, however, artists became more and more bored and increasingly turned their attention to shocking the bourgeoisie. With the rise of ideological art movements, such as Dada or surrealism around the time of the First World War, the arts began to approach the truly absurd: "Objects out of the ordinary environment of modern life were selected and exhibited in the Dada shows as works of art. Duchamp, with serene impudence, mocked serious artistic intention with chance selections of objects like a bicycle wheel, bottle washer, urinal, corkscrew, and other 'ready-made,' commonplace objects. These Andre Breton called 'manufactured objects promoted to the dignity of objects of art through the choice of the artist.'"[129]

With regard to the urinal mentioned here, Marcel Duchamp made this famous (or infamous) submission of it to a New York exhibition in 1917. He called it *The Fountain*. But it was merely a urinal that Duchamp had purchased from a plumbing supply house. As a matter of fact, the submission was rejected by the exhibition managers, but who was to say that it was not art? If art has no purpose and is not part of the complex of human social life, it can now be anything at all. Just as sexual activity, when it loses its connection with its social role in the transmission of human life, may now become anything that is erotically pleasing to the participants.

What I called just now the *ideological art movements*—cubism, futurism, Dada, surrealism, and others—approached art not as a means of adorning and completing man's social

---

[129] Helen Gardner, *Art though the Ages*, 8th ed. (San Diego: Harcourt, Brace, Jovanovich, 1986), 925.

activities, or even as an effort to seek pure beauty, but as an ideology or philosophy. And generally these movements issued manifestos trumpeting their new conceptions of art. The Futurist Technical Manifesto, for example, of 1910 declared, "That all forms of imitation must be despised, all forms of originality glorified." Or as embodied in some Dada slogans from Berlin in 1920,

> DADA stands on the side of the revolutionary
>   Proletariat
> Open up at last your head
> Leave it free for the demands of our age
> Down with art
> Down with bourgeois intellectualism
> Art is dead
> Long live the machine art of Tatlin
> DADA is the voluntary destruction of the bourgeois
>   world of ideas[130]

Now one might wonder how all this new type of art was to pay for itself. Not every artist was content to live an impoverished existence in his garret. I noted before that traditionally whoever was to pay for the artwork exercised some control over its form. So who was going to pay for the creations of Dada or Futurism, especially since the artists themselves were not shy about proclaiming their utter disdain for the bourgeoisie, the only remaining class with enough money to finance such a vast project? Richard Huelsenbeck, one of the Dada theorists,

---

[130] As quoted in Herschel B. Chipp, *Theories of Modern Art* (Berkeley: University of California, 1968), 376.

in 1920 indicated his disdain for middle-class society, writing of the "fat and utterly uncomprehending Zurich philistines that we regarded as pigs" and of "the bourgeois, in whom we saw our mortal enemy."[131] And most of the bourgeois reciprocated by ignoring the fine arts and excluding them from the ordinary activities of their life. But with one important exception. There were always enough of the bourgeoisie who, out of a desire to feel superior to others, or to show that they weren't really bourgeois, were ready to patronize these artists, to pay large sums for ugly or ordinary objects masquerading as art. These, together with museum curators, academics, art journalists, and the artists themselves, now became what is known as the "arts community" and have presumed a right to

---

[131] Richard Huelsenbeck, *En Avant Dada*, 1920, as quoted in Herschel B. Chipp, *Theories of Modern Art*, 377, 378. Previously in this book, I quoted Christopher Dawson's unfavorable remarks on the bourgeois and bourgeois culture. Does this mean that Dawson shares the perspective of these disaffected artists? While the subject is too large to go into detail about here, a couple of things can be said. One is that, as Dawson put it, "Let us admit that it is no use hunting for the bourgeois. For we are all more or less bourgeois and our civilization is bourgeois from top to bottom." Christopher Dawson, "Catholics and the Bourgeois Mind," in *The Dynamics of World History* (La Salle, IL: Sherwood Sugden, 1978), 200. In other words, the avant-garde artists of the 1920s were as much a part of the bourgeoisie as were the Zurich merchants or bankers whom they despised. Had genuine peasants with a pre-bourgeois outlook ever encountered the products of Dada or futurism, the peasants' reactions would have ranged from amused puzzlement to fury, and the artists would have found not allies, but a new set of enemies. A like process takes place when some uneducated but sane janitor in a museum mistakes some modernist art object for trash and discards it. Secondly, in fact, the aesthetic tastes of the bourgeois had been degraded, but degraded precisely by the very historical process that separated art from life and produced, on the one hand, mass-culture art products and, on the other, what I have called the ideological artistic movements, such as Dada.

pronounce on what is and isn't art, who is and isn't a serious artist, and so on. Whereas formerly ordinary people would commission a work of art and, most importantly, would feel qualified to make a judgment about it, now only members of the "arts community" regarded themselves as having anything important to say about art. And, naturally, those who dissented from the generally accepted standards and judgments, those who might actually presume to label a work as ugly or stupid, were banished immediately from the polite society of the artists and their hangers-on. Aside from having sufficient money, the only other criterion for membership in the "arts community" was a willingness to disregard common sense and ordinary healthy aesthetic judgments.

Similar trends occurred even in architecture, the art that everyone realizes has an obvious link with ordinary life. Since architects design buildings in which people actually worship and live and work, it is impossible to disconnect it from the larger activities of life. And so, just as in the other arts, formerly architecture was practiced as part of man's social life as a whole. Those who were to pay for a new building still expected to exercise some control over the finished product. As Tom Wolfe pointed out,

> In the past, those who commissioned and paid for palazzi, cathedrals, opera houses, libraries, universities, museums, ministries, pillared terraces, and winged villas didn't hesitate to turn them into visions of their own glory. Napoleon wanted to turn Paris into Rome under the Caesars, only with louder music and more marble. And it was done. . . . His nephew Napoleon

III wanted to turn Paris into Rome with Versailles piled on top, and it was done. . . . Palmerston once threw out the results of a design competition for a new British Foreign Office building and told the leading Gothic Revival architect of the day, Gilbert Scott, to do it in the Classical style. And Scott did it, because Palmerston said do it.[132]

But because the arts were becoming increasingly devoid of any social purpose, even architecture, to a remarkable extent, became divorced from its social role. Over the course of the twentieth century, the so-called International style, originally formulated in the German architectural school called the *Bauhaus*, became so prominent that thousands of ugly and even impractical buildings were built, all in thrall to a conception of architecture divorced from any humane understanding of social life as a whole.[133]

To take one example which Wolfe details, here is his description of the campus of the Illinois Institute of Technology, built in the 1940s, and designed by Ludwig Mies van der Rohe, who had taught at the Bauhaus itself: "The main classroom building looked like a shoe factory. The chapel looked like a power plant. The power plant itself, also designed by Mies, looked rather more spiritual . . . thanks to its chimney, which reached heavenward at least. The school

---

[132] From Tom Wolfe's insightful and witty account of twentieth-century architecture *From Bauhaus to Our House* (Pocket Books edition, 1982), 9–10.
[133] As regards impractical buildings, Wolfe notes what happened to the Hartford Civic Center coliseum, built with flat roofs, according to the dictum that "pitched roofs were bourgeois." But not taking account of the amount of snowfall in Connecticut, the roofs collapsed. Wolfe, 75.

of architecture building had black steel trusses rising up through the roof on either side of the main entrance, after the manner of a Los Angeles car wash. All four were glass and steel boxes."[134]

Most readers have probably seen more than one Catholic church designed in a similar style, and hopelessly unable to fulfill the purpose of a church building to assist in raising the soul toward God and the things of God. But so much prestige does the "arts community" have that few have the intellectual integrity or the moral courage to challenge it. So they simply shut up and pay up. Unlike in medieval times when Catholic churches took over a hundred years to build with the finest craftsmanship, the richest marble, and the most splendid stained-glass windows, many churches today reflect a culture of economic activity—that is, to construct as quickly and cheaply as possible. Or at the same time, constructing a giant mega Protestant church with a movie theatre and gymnasium that resembles a mall, not a house of God. But there is something deeper here. It takes us back to Judas, who was upset that Mary waisted the precious ointment on the Lord rather than give it to the poor (see Jn 12:3–6). Today, the prosperity preachers and even some bishops would rather have the faithful's funds be spent on their salaries, their large mansions, or their diocesan bureaucracies than truly building a temple for God, a cathedral worthy of God Himself.

As in the other themes mentioned in this book, the fate of the arts in the last century hinges on their loss of connection

---

[134] Wolfe, 65.

with the rest of the life of society. When some particular activity or institution is removed from any connection with a hierarchy of actions, a hierarchy which directs everything to its proper place, then it loses its inherent purpose and becomes whatever any individual wants it to be. Sexuality, political authority, economic activity, artistic creation—they all become simply examples of Justice Kennedy's dictum that allows each one of us to "to define one's own concept of existence, of meaning, of the universe, and of the mystery of human life." Divorced from their own natures, they are necessarily divorced from God, who created those natures. There exists now no meaning, nor purpose, except as a contrivance of the human will, and, in the end, of the wills of those who exercise the most power.

CHAPTER EIGHT

The Environment: Natural and Human

In his encyclical *Centesimus Annus*, Pope Saint John Paul II wrote, "In addition to the irrational destruction of the natural environment, we must also mention the more serious destruction of the *human environment*, something which is by no means receiving the attention it deserves. Although people are rightly worried—though much less than they should be—about preserving the natural habitats of the various animal species threatened with extinction, . . . too little effort is made to *safeguard the moral conditions for an authentic 'human ecology.'*"[135] Two environments, two ecologies. In studying these two environments, we will soon discover that our treatment of the first is related to our treatment of the second.

The problem of the natural environment is familiar to everyone. Whatever may be one's position with regard to any specific question, it seems impossible to deny man's deleterious impact on the natural environment in which God has placed us. This is or should be a concern to us because we have been given only one earth, and if we render it less

---

[135] Pope John Paul II, *Centesimus Annus* (May 1, 1991), no. 38.

habitable or even uninhabitable because of a shortsighted lust for profits or comfort, we have been very foolish indeed. But beyond this, as Christians we should remember that God looked upon "everything that he had made, and behold, it was very good" (Gn 1:31). We can hardly claim to be doing God's will if we disparage or mistreat one of the most beautiful works of His hands.

But the environmental question remains controversial. This is the result of several factors, one of which is the false choices often presented to us. The environmental problem is often posed as a conflict between human beings and other species of living things. It is said that environmentalists care more about snail darters or about the planet itself than they do about the human species and human lives. And sometimes, sadly, this is true. Certain environmental ideologies do exist which downplay both the uniqueness and the primacy of mankind, which have no difficulty with aborting unborn human babies while at the same time lamenting the loss of any small and seemingly insignificant animal population.[136] Of course, such ideologies must be rejected as false. But even though God has placed man at the head of His visible creation, this does not mean that we have been given license to do whatever we want with the natural environment. In fact, it should be obvious that even if we have absolutely no concern for any species but

---

[136] Aristotle wrote with regard to creatures that would seem to have no intrinsic interest for us, "For if some [animals] have no graces to charm the sense, yet even these, by disclosing to intellectual perception the artistic spirit that designed them, give immense pleasure to all who can trace links of causation, and are inclined to philosophy." *On the Parts of Animals* 1.5.

our own, still if we pollute the earth or the atmosphere excessively, we will eventually harm ourselves. Just as no one but a fool would allow his house or apartment to be littered with waste or junk, so we must think of the earth as our home, for it certainly is that.

An often overlooked approach to existing with a minimum of harm to our surroundings is the idea of living *with* the natural world. Too often the choice is presented as one of domination of the environment or of uncritical surrender to those who appear to insist that the ideal would be to live as hunter gatherers. But there is another way. We human beings do have the right from God to use and alter the natural environment, to eat plants and animals and otherwise make use of them. But we do not have the right to do this in just any way we please. We should not make animals suffer more than is necessary nor for trivial purposes. As much as possible, we should seek out farming methods that respect the integrity of God's creation, instead of seeing our activity as an opportunity to exercise our *will*, our sense of domination over the largely helpless creation which God has placed at our feet and entrusted to our care. Too often modern men are not "respectful students, custodians, and assistants of nature, who learn to work with it for our good and for the good of the whole, but rapists who overpower nature for their own pleasure, slave-drivers who subject creatures to their own wills."[137]

---

[137] Peter Kwasniewski, "Listening with an Attentive Ear to God's Poetry," in Thomas Storck, ed., *The Glory of the Cosmos: A Catholic Approach to the Natural World* (Waterloo, ON: Arouca Press, 2020), 143.

We have already seen that the new kind of science which arose following the collapse of the Christian civilization of the Middle Ages has fostered such attitudes toward the natural world. This world is seen primarily as something which exists solely for our material benefit and, at the same time, has been divested of its inherent worth and is regarded, as in Descartes's philosophy, as simply a shapeless mass of stuff. This is in contrast with the philosophy of Aristotle and Saint Thomas, which recognized that each living thing, no matter how small, has a nature of its own, lovingly created by God. And that each such nature, in its own way, praises God simply by existing and fulfilling its own purpose, apart from any use that we might make of it, as we can see in the beautiful hymn of praise in the Old Testament book of Daniel, chapter three, which calls upon the sun and the moon, upon the stars, even upon showers of rain and the dew and winds and fire and cold, light and darkness, lightning and clouds, and upon the earth itself to bless the Lord. If we recognize these truths, then while we will not cease to make use of and enjoy the natural world around us, we will cease to exploit it, to use it for trivial purposes, to act as if only our aims were important, and that if we are intending to eat any particular animal, then it does not matter how we treat it beforehand or what method we use to kill it. For we cannot plead that since the natural world exists in great part for man's use, therefore anything we want to do with it is legitimate. It exists for our reasonable use, not our exploitation. We are invited to collaborate with it, to make use of its inherent powers, not to seek to wrest and twist them to whatever is our will.

In our very ownership of the land there does not exist an unrestricted right to do anything we like with it. No individual human person will live forever on this earth, and if we forget about the generations that are to come after us, then we have presumed a status as lords of this world that is not ours. Property in land is essentially different from other types of property, for the amount of land can hardly be increased. It is a finite gift of God. So if, for example, someone were to pave over needed farmland with absolutely no thought for the future agricultural needs of humanity, he would surely sin by his misuse of the earth which God has given to all of us.[138] No single generation has the right to elevate its own profits and pleasures at the expense of generations to come.

As serious as are our obligations with regard to the natural environment, John Paul speaks of "the more serious destruction of the *human environment.*" But are these two unrelated questions or do they both stem from a common origin or, rather, from a common sort of mentality? The connection between the two concerns something that Pope Francis discussed in his 2015 encyclical *Laudato Si'*, what he called the technological imperative. What is that?

Francis set forth the basic points of his exposition as follows:

> Humanity has taken up technology and its development *according to an undifferentiated and one-dimensional paradigm.* This paradigm exalts the concept of a subject who, using logical and rational procedures, progressively approaches and gains control over an external

---

[138] Cf. Leo XIII, *Rerum Novarum* (May 15, 1891), no. 8.

object. This subject makes every effort to establish the scientific and experimental method, which in itself is already a technique of possession, mastery, and transformation. . . . Men and women have constantly intervened in nature, but for a long time this meant being in tune with and respecting the possibilities offered by the things themselves. It was a matter of receiving what nature itself allowed, as if from its own hand. Now, by contrast, we are the ones to lay our hands on things, attempting to extract everything possible from them while frequently ignoring or forgetting the reality in front of us. Human beings and material objects no longer extend a friendly hand to one another; the relationship has become confrontational. This has made it easy to accept the idea of infinite or unlimited growth, which proves so attractive to economists, financiers, and experts in technology.[139]

And in the next section, the pope notes the "tendency . . . to make the method and aims of science and technology an epistemological paradigm"; that is, the very way we think is encompassed within this approach, and only with difficulty can we learn to see things otherwise. Francis continues, echoing John Paul II and pointing out that "the effects of this model on reality as a whole, human and social, are seen in the deterioration of the environment, but this is just one sign of a reductionism which affects every aspect of human and social life."[140]

---

[139] Pope Francis, *Laudato Si'* (May 24, 2015), no. 106.
[140] Pope Francis, no. 107.

If, then, Francis links his concern for the natural environment with "human and social life," we can now examine more closely John Paul's concern for "the *human environment*" and see more clearly the link between these two ecologies of creation. John Paul mentions the following as some of the matters of concern when dealing with this created reality of the human environment: "the serious problems of modern urbanization," "*the family*," and "the production and consumption of goods [as] the center of social life and society's only value."[141]

How does what Francis calls the "technological imperative" affect such human and social realities? We will be able to understand this if we realize that the "technological imperative" deals with more than technology in the narrow sense—that is, with machines, devices, physical systems, and so on. In fact, it is a fundamental way of looking at reality. It "exalts the concept of a subject who, using logical and rational procedures, progressively approaches and gains control over an external object." It is a technique of control, and can be applied just as easily to human activities—and indeed to human beings themselves—as to the natural world.

Take the example of the family which John Paul II notes. Certainly today families face many problems, such as isolation from the kinds of extended family networks that once supported and assisted fathers and mothers, economic problems, problems with access to an education that respects human values, and many more. But what solutions does society offer, based on its own "logical and rational procedures"

---

[141] Pope John Paul II, *Centesimus Annus*, nos. 38, 39.

that seek to gain control "over an external object"? If a family needs support beyond the physical resources of mother and father, then daycare appears as an easy answer. If there is an economic problem such as limited access to housing or insufficient income, the logical techniques of artificial contraception or even abortion are offered as obvious and easy solutions. If conflicts arise between spouses, divorce is ready at hand to eliminate all such difficulties.

The logic here is not one of respecting the nature of the institution or activity with which one is dealing—marriage and the family—according to its own nature and inherent purpose, but of applying a technological solution that, like too many technological solutions, appears to offer some technique, some process, that eliminates the problem quickly and with little effort. Healing a marriage, for example, can be difficult, while divorce is a quick and attractive final solution. Adjusting our economy so that fathers can support their families on one income requires not only hard thinking but considerable good will; promoting contraceptives is an easy fix that allows us to leave the underlying economic distortion untouched, and incidentally makes a good profit for pharmaceutical companies.

Unfortunately, we can observe an even more extreme application of the technological imperative. Today, an increasing number of persons, both male and female, are claiming to discover that they are in fact of a different sex from the one indicated by their bodies. And as in other matters, a remedy is ready to hand: the surgical and chemical mutilation of their bodies in accordance with their assertion of what is their true sex. If mental illness is a disconnect between perception and reality, then surely a disconnect that puts the reality of one's own body in question is a perfect example of a mental disorder. We should not doubt that in many cases people do suffer from the feeling that they were "assigned" to the wrong sex or trapped in the wrong sort of body. Such persons deserve our sympathy and help. And as in many mental illnesses, treatment can be difficult and uncertain. How much easier it is to grab the tools offered by the technological imperative. If we wonder how such a thing as transgenderism could be so readily accepted, then we should look to our prior adherence to technology as simply a quick and easy way of dealing with what appear to be simple problems. Technology offers the way out, a much easier way than trying to correct or improve the human environment as a whole.

The technological imperative has thoroughly shaped our civilization and way of life. It has affected our education and, as a result, the very way we learn to think. By dividing knowledge into increasingly smaller spheres, we make it harder for someone to approach a problem or difficulty in a holistic manner. *Laudato Si'* again: "The specialization which belongs to technology makes it difficult to see the larger picture. The fragmentation of knowledge proves helpful for concrete applications, yet it often leads to a loss of appreciation for the whole, for the relationships between things, and for the broader horizon, which then becomes irrelevant."[142]

For someone whose training has created an outlook that sees each difficulty as a discrete problem to be "solved" by some technique, then a technique such as contraception as

---

[142] Pope Francis, *Laudato Si'*, no. 110.

the answer to family financial concerns becomes almost irresistible. What could possibly be wrong with it? Do we not approach all of the problems and difficulties that we encounter in life in the same manner? We see a discrete problem—well, here is a discrete solution. You want to go from point X to point Y faster and more securely—why here is a motor car, it will do the trick. Never mind what the overall effects might be on society, on human life, on the human and natural environments, even on our chances of attaining eternal life.

As in the many issues discussed in this book, it is the lack of a vision of the whole, a vision necessarily hierarchical in nature, with God at the apex, that makes thinking according to the technological imperative seem like second nature to us. It has affected our entire civilization. In fact, we assume that it is the natural and only way to think and to act, to approach problems and to solve them. The fact that a "solution" according to the technological imperative usually causes even more problems does not disturb anyone very much, for the same technique is at hand to deal with these new problems. We usually can find some further discrete and direct way of doing so, and we then start the entire process over again. And again and again. Our life and society become an endless series of problems that we try to fix by our repeated application of techniques "of possession, mastery, and transformation." But unless we can recover the ability to look at life and society as a whole, the separate and disparate activities and fields of human endeavor will never rest in the harmonious unity that points our entire earthly life toward the heavenly kingdom and helps us to pass through temporal goods so as not to lose the eternal.

CHAPTER NINE

Recapitulation

The topics we have looked at in this volume are those that lie at the roots of our cultural separation from the Gospel. They exemplify the consequences of the Protestant principle of private judgment, joined to the equally influential and noxious Lockean principle that religion, at least in its dogmatic aspects, is a purely private affair, and that the civic and social order is to be officially agnostic. While originally this may have seemed to some a sensible way of avoiding the religious strife that had brought repeated wars and persecutions to Europe for 150 years and more, when erected into a fundamental political principle, it led inexorably to something like Justice Anthony Kennedy's dictum that "at the heart of liberty is the right to define one's own concept of existence, of meaning, of the universe, and of the mystery of human life."

As the Catholic tradition unequivocally asserts, it is natural for mankind to live in community, for not only will we lack many necessary physical things, but more importantly, we will also be unable to develop ourselves intellectually and culturally outside of a political community. Thus it is a contradiction of the deepest kind to say that that community must have no concern for the fundamental questions that should preoccupy men's minds, for the *mystery* that lies at the heart of every human culture, for our concept of God and of how to please Him, and of our destiny beyond this life. For it is a fact, however we might explain it, that individuals pass beyond this life—but pass into what? The atheist must contend with the fact that the only being who inhabits this earth and who is able to rise above his environment in order to ponder all things in heaven and earth and below the earth, that this being passes away in death, that our human minds, so wonderfully made, apparently cease to exist. What meaning is there in this? What cruel and blind evolutionary process brought such a being into existence and then at length destroys him?

The atheist might throw up his hands and say he knows not why or how, but the religious believer, particularly the Catholic, who is in possession of the true Faith, should know that these questions are of such immense importance that they are more than private matters. They are more than the private musing of individuals who are all on their way to final extinction. No, they are of the very business of human living, and therefore of the human community in which God has created us to live. If we do not recognize that, then we are, whether we realize it or not, committed to the radical and subjective individualism of Justice Kennedy.

If, then, a concern for the ultimate meaning of things is proper not just to us as individuals but to us as a community, then the importance of the many topics discussed in this book should be clear. Whether as a community we engage ourselves with these questions, or whether we try to ignore them, we will construct a society that reflects our decision. Hence, for us, the various aspects of human life and the institutions that surround them reflect our decision to privatize religion and, as a result, to separate what we consider the real business of human life from God.

These decisions have played out in many areas, as we have seen. Indeed, there are topics not explicitly discussed in this book but derived from the principles that I have striven to explain and illustrate. For example, our national preoccupation with sports, disfigured by money, and whose effects on education I have already discussed, has taken an innocent and essentially healthy love of games and physical exercise and transformed it into a gigantic financial colossus. Or on a more personal level, how have the modest food portions and drink sizes of 1950s America grown into thirty-two-ounce containers and super-sized meals? Or in an even more direct perversion of our natural desire for food, do all-you-can-eat restaurants or buffets serve to sustain our bodily health or do they directly undermine it? What do such features of our collective life say about the ultimate orientation of our culture, about our approach to the "mystery of God"?

If the Prosperity Gospel is recognized as the absurdity that it is, is it not equally absurd to habitually go beyond our natural bodily needs in eating and drinking, even to create establishments whose very reason for existence is to cater to such diseased appetites? Recall the words of Saint Thomas that I quoted earlier, that "the appetite of natural riches is not infinite, because according to a set measure they satisfy nature; but the appetite of artificial riches is infinite, because it serves inordinate concupiscence."[143] If eating has a purpose, then to consistently violate that purpose by excess is to overturn the inherent purpose of eating.

In his encyclical *Centesimus Annus*, Pope Saint John Paul II declared how "the affluent society or the consumer society" showed the "failure of Marxism to contribute to a humane and better society," insofar as Communist states were often unable to supply the basic material goods that mankind needs. But on a deeper level, the affluent society, "insofar as it denies an autonomous existence and value to morality, law, culture and religion, it agrees with Marxism, in the sense that it totally reduces man to the sphere of economics and the satisfaction of material needs."[144]

As seen throughout this book, most of the distortions of human life that we have examined are of this nature; that is, they reduce "man to the sphere of economics and the satisfaction of material needs." Or, even worse, to the disordered satisfaction of human appetites well beyond satisfaction of any possible material needs.

Perceptive readers of this book might have noticed that, historically speaking, the distortions of human life that have occurred in the last several hundred years have proceeded from the outside toward the inside of the human person. It was the economic and political orders which first became disordered and detached from their respective purposes. Then the attack was launched against the family, with the promotion of divorce, contraception, and then abortion.

---

[143] Thomas Aquinas, *Summa Theologiae* (Westminister, MD: Christian Classics, 1981), I-II, q. 2, a. 1, ad 3.
[144] Pope John Paul II, *Centesimus Annus* (May 1, 1991), no. 19.

Finally, in our days, the very stuff of human nature and our very bodies are subjected to an astounding assault. It is claimed that the contours and functions of the body are meaningless, always subject to claims that a disordered or diseased mind is apt to make, so that a man can think he is a woman, or a woman a man, and physically or chemically mutilate their bodies in a vain attempt to overturn reality. Not only is this a prime instance of the application of the technological imperative, but it shows clearly that when our fundamental principles begin to unravel, there is no natural stopping point. Not only is this because all aspects of human life are logically connected so that when one area is attacked, the other areas suffer.

Behind these attacks on the human society and the human person is not some harmless distorted gospel message of prosperity. No, it is Satan himself, who is working from the outside inward and has managed to bring huge swathes of human life and activity under his sway. But only if we can begin to understand what has happened can we begin to work to undo it. Whether we will be successful or not is of much less importance than whether we have set our minds to understand the trajectory of events and to take steps, however small, to renew all things in Christ.

Epilogue

"For what doth it profit a man, if he gain the whole world, and suffer the loss of his own soul?" (Matt. 16:26, DV). In a sense, this entire book has been a meditation on this question. How we shape our individual lives, how we shape the society of which we are necessarily parts and which in turn has such an enormous impact on how we think and live. These are the questions we must consider if we are to obtain eternal life which is the proper end of man. Our life on earth is a complicated network and complex of activities, institutions, and practices which develop according to some ruling idea, fundamentally a religious idea: "At the heart of every culture lies the attitude a person takes to the greatest mystery: the mystery of God. Different cultures are basically different ways of facing the question of the meaning of personal existence,"[145] as Pope John Paul wrote and as I have quoted more than once.

A reader of these pages might conclude that the varying evils and misuses of so many things presented here concern society as a whole rather than the individual believer. That somehow these are not *my* problems, but rather problems of the social order to be solved at a level higher than myself. That we as individual persons are more victims than participants in them. In a certain sense, this is true. Most of us do

---

[145] Pope John Paul II, *Centesimus Annus* (May 1, 1991), no. 24.

not fully realize how much we are shaped by the society in which we live and have been formed, how we have taken in our attitudes from our parents, our schooling, and from the countless customs, activities, institutions, and processes that surround us. The anthropologist Alfred Kroeber described the situation we are in as follows:

> The degree to which every individual is molded by his culture is enormous. . . . The formal or deliberate part of the process we call education: education through schools, in religion, and in manners, and morals primarily at home. These agencies convey the mores and some of the folkways. But perhaps a larger fraction of the cultural tradition is acquired by each individual at his own initiative. . . . In this class are his speech, bodily postures and gestures, mental and social attitudes, which he imitates from his elders or from near-age mates, and a thousand and one activities . . . which a child "learns," often without any formal instruction, because he has seen others do these things and wants to do them too.[146]

Hence my efforts to show how the roots of the Prosperity Gospel lie deep in our culture and are nourished by ideas that are at the heart of a Protestant understanding of Christianity. We are definitely parts of a greater whole. However, such a conclusion would be partial and not entirely correct since it is our own souls, our own lives, our own families that are being

---

[146] Alfred Kroeber, *Anthropology: Culture Patterns and Processes* (New York: Harcourt, Brace & World, 1963), 96.

impacted, and we bear a significant responsibility for allowing ourselves to imbibe erroneous and evil ideas into our own lives and that of our families. We can make efforts not only to look critically on the society around us but to preserve ourselves and our families from at least its most egregious excesses and errors. We may be significantly influenced by our cultures, but we are not altogether trapped within them.

For it is more than at the heart of each culture that there lies a mystery. Within each individual human heart there is also a mystery, a personal mystery, the mystery of the fundamental orientation of each of us. Is that mystery toward God or toward some idol we have erected in place of God? It is we ourselves who make decisions and choices about the acquisition and consumption of material goods. We decide whether we will prefer material goods to spiritual or intellectual goods, a larger house and a newer car, or a more expensive vacation, to perhaps one more child. Though the demands of living in a particular society can be overwhelming and hard to resist, it is always true that we have *some* choice in what we buy, in whether we acquire the latest gadgets or make do, if we can, with an older version. To realize the immense impact that society exercises does not absolve us of all responsibility.

But if it is indeed God whom we have placed at the center of our hearts, then, perhaps gradually but eventually, all the multitudinous things of earth and earthly life will arrange themselves in a hierarchy according to the place that God intends for them in the scheme of human life and society. They will serve the purposes that both God's intention and their own inherent natures indicate. We will then never lose our way while traveling this earth. For any way we might tread upon will always be the way to our heavenly home.

How then can we ourselves contribute to a right use and ordering of created goods? In our own personal relations with God, with the faith, hope, and charity that we try to exercise in His name, we can strive to realize that they have implications beyond simply our individual lives, or even the lives of our families. In fact, we can try to link up our individual efforts with those of the entire Church, and even with the good that is exercised or has been attained in our society as a whole. We are necessarily, according to our nature, members of society; we make use of created goods in fulfilling our needs and the needs of our neighbors; we create or at least make use of technology; we learn or educate the next generation, and so on. No one of these spheres of human activity is indifferent as to its shape and purpose. Each can reflect better or worse the divine order which God intends for human life even on this earth. The *human environment*, as Pope Saint John Paul II called it, is something which has a profound effect on our lives, even on our attainment of eternal life. It is worth our time and efforts to shape it properly. We do not do well if we regard it with indifference, believing that only our existence as individuals has significance.

Moreover, we do not need to confront the stark choices of either social compliance or individual or family nonconformity. We are members of parishes and often related to one or more other intermediate groups. It is possible to foster a spirit of Catholic living among such groups, a spirit which can assist its members in collectively resisting the dictates of the culture around us.

The Prosperity Gospel is absurd, yes. But its very absurdity shows us the length to which our conceptions of life on this earth can depart from the ways of God and pursue instead false appearances of the good. Or rather, a valuation of material goods that is false. Wealth, health, thriving relationships—none of these is evil in itself. But all quickly incline toward evil when their pursuit is separated from that hierarchy of goods which I have mentioned so many times in this book. "Apart from me, you can do nothing," said Our Lord (Jn 15:5). And apart from Him, we can even say, nothing really *is*, for only the things that have been brought into this hierarchy will have lasting significance, in one fashion or another, into eternity, and will form part of our enjoyment of God. If our marriages, our families, and even our civic lives have been conducted according to their rightful place in the divine framework, then they will surely be part of our eternal happiness. If not, they will be, at best, matters to be expiated in the purgatorial fire and, at worst, something to be endured in the more grievous fires of hell.

In a striking passage, Saint Paul admonishes us to a detachment from the good things of this world: "I mean, brethren, the appointed time has grown very short; from now on, let those who have wives live as though they had none, and those who mourn as though they were not mourning, and those who rejoice as though they were not rejoicing, and those who buy as though they had no goods, and those who deal with the world as though they had no dealings with it" (1 Cor 7:29–31).

It is clear from many other places in Saint Paul's writings that he does not mean for this to be understood literally.

Yet, in another sense, it *is* meant literally if we realize that we never possess the goods of this world—even our own spouses—absolutely, but always subject to God's will as that is revealed in the events and even afflictions of this world. With riches, we do need to be detached, otherwise they will possess us and can even lead to the loss of our salvation. We can possess the riches of this world, we can make use of them, but we should cultivate a sense of fear and trembling as we handle something which has led many, as Saint Paul put it, "into temptation, into a snare, into many senseless and hurtful desires that plunge men into ruin and destruction" (1 Tm 6:9). Hence we may rightly speak of a spirit of evangelical or voluntary poverty even for those who are not bound by vows of poverty and whose life requires the possession and use of external goods. All of us must strive to achieve a level of detachment from these things, not because they are evil, but because, due to our fallen state, we are always prone to misuse them and give our hearts to them.

Pope Saint Paul VI spoke of the separation between the Gospel and culture in his apostolic exhortation *Evangelii Nuntiandi*:

> Evangelization is to be achieved, not from without as though by adding some decoration or applying a coat of colour, but in depth, going to the very centre and roots of life. The gospel must impregnate the culture and the whole way of life of man. . . .
>
> The rift between the gospel and culture is undoubtedly an unhappy circumstance of our times just as it has been in other eras. Accordingly we must devote all

Epilogue

Epilogue

153

our resources and all our efforts to the sedulous evan-
gelization of human culture, or rather of the various
human cultures. They must be regenerated through
contact with the gospel.[147]

This is the separation "between the gospel and culture" that
has allowed our culture to become so deformed in so many
ways. But as Catholics, we can make an effort to change this,
to make not only our individual lives but also our whole
society, our culture, reflect the divine hierarchy according to
which everything is ordered to God. As Pope Pius XI wrote
of the economic order, but in words which could as easily be
applied to any other aspect of human society,

For it is the moral law alone which commands us to
seek in all our conduct our supreme and final end,
and to strive directly in our specific actions for those
ends which nature, or rather, the Author of Nature,
has established for them, duly subordinating the particular to the general. If this law be faithfully obeyed,
the result will be that particular economic aims,
whether of society as a body or of individuals, will be
intimately linked with the universal teleological order,
and as a consequence we shall be led by progressive
stages to the final end of all, God Himself, our highest
and lasting good.[148]

The Epistle to the Hebrews in the New Testament tells us
that "here we have no lasting city, but we seek the city which

---

[147] Pope Paul VI, *Evangelii Nuntiandi* (December 8, 1975), no. 20.
[148] Pope Pius XI, *Quadragesimo Anno* (May 15, 1931), no. 43.

is to come" (13:14). We must live in this world knowing that not only will we ourselves pass out of it but this world itself will come to an end. The goods that we strive to acquire and preserve here will, in themselves, have no meaning in the life to come. Either we will enjoy God and find our sufficiency in Him or we will be eternally separated from that joy. But if we have tried to use the good things of this life in an ordered fashion, then they will have some lasting meaning for us even when we pass beyond this world. Even in the midst of a culture dedicated to its own destruction, a culture obsessed with prosperity, the choice still remains for us how we may pass through temporal goods so as not to lose the eternal: that *transeamus per bona temporalia, ut non amittamus aeterna.* May it please God that we use the things of this world in such a manner that we do reach our eternal reward.